Paul–Shackled and Shipwrecked!

Group

Loveland, Colorado

www.group.com

Group resources actually work!

This Group resource helps you focus on **"The 1 Thing™"**— a life-changing relationship with Jesus Christ. "The 1 Thing" incorporates our **R.E.A.L.** approach to ministry. It reinforces a growing friendship with Jesus, encourages long-term learning, and results in life transformation, because it's:

Relational
Learner-to-learner interaction enhances learning and builds Christian friendships.

Experiential
What learners experience through discussion and action sticks with them up to 9 times longer than what they simply hear or read.

Applicable
The aim of Christian education is to equip learners to be both hearers and doers of God's Word.

Learner-based
Learners understand and retain more when the learning process takes into consideration how they learn best.

BibleVenture Centers™: Paul—Shackled and Shipwrecked!
Copyright © 2005 Group Publishing, Inc.

Visit our Web site: **www.group.com**

Credits

Author: Jan Kershner
Creative Development Editor: Mikal Keefer
Chief Creative Officer: Joani Schultz
Copy Editor: Lyndsay E. Gerwing
Art Director/Designer: Helen H. Harrison
Illustrator: Matt Wood
Cover Art Director/Designer: Bambi Eitel
Cover Illustrator: Patty O'Friel
Production Manager: Peggy Naylor

Library of Congress Cataloging-in-Publication Data
Paul, shackled and shipwrecked!-- 1st American pbk.
   p. cm. -- (BibleVenture centers)
  ISBN 0-7644-2794-6 (pbk. : alk. paper)
  1. Paul, the Apostle, Saint--Study and teaching. 2. Bible. N.T. Acts--Study and teaching. 3. Christian education of children. I. Group Publishing. II. Series.

  BS2506.3.P384 2004
  225.9'2--dc22

                    2004015119

10 9 8 7 6 5 4 3 2 1   14 13 12 11 10 09 08 07 06 05
Printed in the United States of America.

Contents

Welcome to BibleVentures™

Ever wish you could connect with *all* your kids, not just the few who seem to naturally enjoy your classroom?

Most Christian educators find themselves wondering why Nancy tracks along with the lesson while Jason is busy poking his neighbors. And why does Darrell light up when it's time to be in a drama, but he'd rather eat worms than do a craft project?

If you've wondered if you're a poor teacher or you have a roomful of aliens, relax. You're dealing with learning styles—and covering all the bases is a challenge every classroom leader faces. You're not alone.

God wired different children differently. That's a good thing—otherwise, we'd live in a world populated solely by mechanical engineers. Or maybe everyone would be an artist and our world would be a dazzling burst of color and music—but the bridges would all fall down.

We *need* to have different people in the world...and in the church.

BibleVentures gives you the opportunity for hands-on exploration of key Bible events using a variety of learning styles. You'll open up the truth of the Bible Point and the Scripture passage to a wide variety of children, whether they learn best through their ears, their fingers, or their eyes. You'll engage children and provide a "wow!" of surprise as kids move from one BibleVenture Center to another.

And best of all, you'll know that you're helping long-term, high-impact learning to happen. Your kids won't just *hear* God's Word; they'll *experience* it. You'll plant it deep in their hearts and minds.

So get ready for a learning adventure. *You'll* know you're providing a balanced, learning experience that taps a range of learning styles, but your kids won't know...or care.

They'll just know they're having a blast learning—and that, in your class, you speak their language.

How to Use This Program

Each week children will gather as one large group at **The Depot**—the launching spot for their weekly adventures. Here they'll experience a fun opening that draws their attention to the Bible Point.

From The Depot, children move with their designated teams to one of the four **Venture Centers.** Children will remain in their Venture Centers for forty minutes and, while there, dive deep into one portion of the Bible story through dramas, games, music, puppets, or other fun activities. Then everyone returns to The Depot for a time of closing and celebration.

Included in your *BibleVentures* book are
- 1 leader's section,
- 1 set of leader job descriptions,
- 4 Venture Center Leaders sections,
- 4 reproducible visa sheets, and
- 1 reproducible CD.

You'll use these resources to lead children on an exciting and interactive four-week journey through the life of Paul!

Also included for your use, should you choose to use them, are
- a sample invitation letter to help you encourage kids in your church and your neighborhood to attend,
- BibleVenture Center Leader encouragers—so your volunteers grow in their commitment in serving kids and Christ,
- a brief article to send to your leaders about how to connect with kids, and
- a teacher training session!

Bible Point Alert!

As children move through this BibleVenture program, they'll discover a foundational Bible truth—a Bible Point. The Bible Point is mentioned often in each Venture Center. Encourage your kids to explore the Bible Point and live it out every day of the week!

Ready to get started? Here's how...

1. Recruit leaders.
You'll need five Venture Center Leaders for this BibleVenture.
One leader will oversee The Depot gatherings. The other four leaders will run the four Venture Centers. Review the different Venture Centers *before* recruiting leaders; that way you'll be able to match up the major learning style used in each center with someone who enjoys connecting with kids in that way.

For instance, if you have a center that uses lots of music, find a bouncy, fun

song leader who loves Jesus and loves kids. If a center uses art to tell a Bible story, ask an artistic, crafty person to lead that center.

One plus of the BibleVenture method of teaching is that teachers get to use their strengths! But that only happens if you're careful to match needs of the centers with the gifts of the teachers.

The person leading The Depot will have new material to present each week, while the Venture Center Leaders will teach one session four times over the course of four weeks. Since a new group of children rotates through the center each week, the leader can use the same lesson four times!

This approach allows for less weekly preparation on the part of your center leaders. And they'll improve from week to week as they fine-tune their presentations.

You'll also need some BibleVenture Buddies.

These are adults or capable teenagers who each befriend a small group of children. We call those small groups "Venture Teams." BibleVenture Buddies hang out with their Venture Teams and serve as a guide, facilitator, and friend.

BibleVenture Buddies don't prepare a lesson or teach. Instead, they get to know their kids. Buddies learn names, pray for the children on their Venture Teams, and reach out to kids in appropriate ways. If Jodie is absent, it's the BibleVenture Buddy who sends a postcard to let her know she was missed. If Jodie is sick, it's her BibleVenture Buddy who calls to encourage her.

BibleVenture Buddies show up for class ten minutes early so they're ready to greet children. They travel with kids to different centers each week and enthusiastically join in to play the games, do the crafts, sing the music, and do whatever else the children do.

Your BibleVenture Buddies aren't teachers, but they help kids connect with the Bible truth being taught in each center. Because they get to know their kids, they're perfectly positioned to help relate the Bible truths to individual kids' lives.

How many BibleVenture Buddies will you need? It depends on how many children participate in your program. For purposes of crowd control and relationship-building, it's best if Venture Teams consist of five to seven children, and you'll need one BibleVenture Buddy for each team. You'll keep the same team of children together throughout your four-week adventure.

And here's a tip for leaders: Look for BibleVenture Buddies among people who *haven't* been Christian education volunteers in the past. Clearly communicate that you're not asking these folks to teach; you're asking them to be a friend to a small group of children. This job is completely *different* from being a Sunday school teacher!

2. Give each leader his or her section of this book.

Don't worry—those sections are reproducible for use in your local church. So is the CD, so ask a teenager in your congregation to burn a copy for each of the leaders. Copying CDs is easy, inexpensive, and—so long as you use the CDs in your church only—completely legal!

Here's how to distribute the pages:

- The Depot: pages 27-51
- Venture Center One: The Drama Center: pages 53-60
- Venture Center Two: The Art Center: pages 61-66
- Venture Center Three: The Games Center: pages 67-74
- Venture Center Four: The Visual Center: pages 75-80

3. Create groups of children.

When you're creating individual Venture Teams, form your teams with children of various ages. This allows older children to help the younger ones and to be role models. It also results in fewer discipline problems.

"What?" you may be thinking. "Not keep all my third-grade girls together? They'll go on strike!"

Trust us: When you create Venture Teams that combine several ages, *especially* if you have an adult volunteer travel with each team, you'll see fewer discipline issues arise. Children may groan a bit at first, but reassure them that they'll be able to hang out with their same-age buddies before the BibleVenture starts.

Besides, when you use mixed-age groupings, you're *also* separating your fifth-grade boys!

Some churches choose to create multi-age groups by combining first-through third-graders and then creating separate groups of fourth- and fifth-graders. This is also an option.

Help children remember what Venture Teams they're in by assigning each team a color. Or get into the theme of this BibleVenture and ask Venture Teams to come up with theme-based names for themselves!

As you assign children to their Venture Teams, make a notation on their name tags and on their BibleVenture Visas as to which team they're on. That way when kids sign in each week at The Depot ticket window, they'll quickly remember what team to join for the remainder of the program.

Be certain each child and adult has a name tag to wear each week. Name tags allow everyone to know each other's names (instead of saying, "You, in the blue shirt."), *and* they allow leaders to know that a child has signed in. You can make permanent name tags that kids and leaders reuse each week or write names on self-stick labels. A quick and easy way for kids to know what teams they're on is to use name tags in colors that correspond to their Venture Teams. Or use white labels and write names in colorful ink that corresponds to Venture Teams.

Please note: Because you have four Venture Centers going at the same time, you need to form four groupings of children to attend them. If you have four Venture Teams, it's easy—just send one team to each Venture Center. If you have more than that, do what you can to have an approximately even number of kids (or teams) in each of the centers. It makes life easier for center leaders if they see about the same number of kids each week.

If you have a smaller number of children—fewer than fifteen—participating in your program, you might consider keeping all the kids together and doing a different Venture Center each week.

4. Make copies of visas.

You'll want a visa for each child in attendance, plus extras for visitors. Visas are distributed the first time you meet, so make copies now and get that task out of the way.

It's perfectly legal for you to make as many copies as you need for your local church use.

5. Walk through the entire BibleVenture with your volunteers.

Invite your leaders to sit down with you and talk through what they'll be doing, when they'll do it, and where they'll be serving. Many leaders like to know where they'll hold their class so they can think through the logistics of how to stage a drama or where to store supplies from week to week.

Besides, you'll want to pray with your team and thank them for loving kids and helping kids discover Bible truths. A quick meeting is one good way to do that.

That's it—five easy steps to memorable, exciting, fun learning! *BibleVentures* is easy—and it's a blast!

During this four-week adventure about the life of Paul, children will learn 2 Corinthians 5:17, which says, "Therefore, if anyone is in Christ, he is a new creation; the old has gone, the new has come!" God dramatically changed Paul from a staunch anti-Christian to a devout follower of Jesus. After meeting Jesus, Paul became a new creation.

God can change us, too. Children will learn and apply this verse through activities in The Depot and in the Venture Centers. Consider creating a poster, banner, or other visual with the Venture Verse on it to display during this BibleVenture.

It's important to note that what you're after isn't just that kids can recite the verse—that wouldn't take more than ten minutes and a stack of candy bar rewards.

What you want is for children to plant the truth of the words deep in their hearts and minds. You want kids to make the connection that the God who changed Paul is the same God who can change them.

That's an empowering truth. A truth that may run counter to what children hear on the playground, in class, and—perhaps—at home.

At BibleVentures you won't have children memorize a blizzard of Scripture passages that will be tucked in their short-term memory today and totally gone tomorrow. Instead, kids will be exposed to the meaning of the words and the impact of the truth of God knowing them, loving them, and wanting to change their lives and help them change their worlds.

If you choose to make Bible memory a larger part of your BibleVenture Center program, great. It's easy to integrate more verses into the program. But remember that when it comes to bringing about true life change, "less is more." It's far better to focus on one verse that sinks deep into how children view themselves before God than to slide a bunch of words into their heads.

The Venture Visas

Make one BibleVenture Visa for each child. Photocopy the BibleVenture Visas on pages 15–19. Place the cover on top and the pages inside in any order—the order isn't important as children can quickly find the appropriate page when asked to do so. And have a visa for each child—kids *love* having their own special visas!

Make it easier for kids to know what teams they're on by having the color of the construction paper for each team be unique and consistent.

Each week children will have their BibleVenture Visas stamped, stickered, or signed by a leader. In this BibleVenture program, that happens at The Depot, in the opening or closing program.

At the closing, BibleVenture Buddies will gather the visas and return them to the leader of The Depot, who'll keep the visas for the following week.

At the last closing, children will receive them to take home.

This visa is the property of

_____

and secures safe transport and assures the bearer admittance to each Venture Center.

This is an area of my life in which I need God's help to change.

Venture Visa

I need God's help in this rocky situation:

The Travel Plan

Use the following chart to help you plan where children will travel each week.

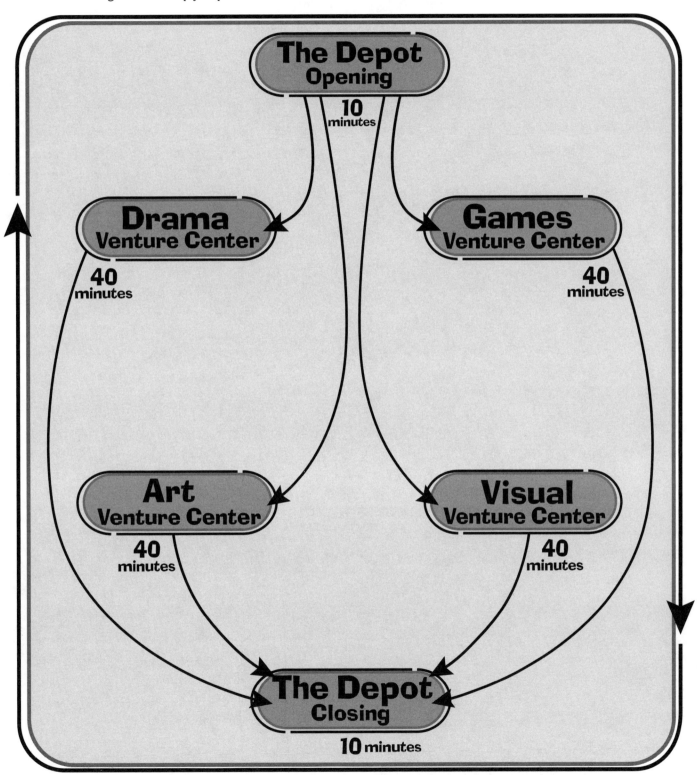

Make the Most of Your BibleVenture

You'll be exploring the life of Paul for four weeks, so make the most of it and have fun with décor and costumes. You can keep it simple with a few posters or go all out and create an entire Bible-times landscape. Picture your leaders wearing costumes, and think what you could accomplish if you recruited a crew with scissors and thread to make simple costumes for all the kids to wear!

Here are some ideas:

Costumes

The basis for most costumes is a tunic. For an easy-make, quick-wear tunic, fold a length of fabric in half and cut a half-circle from the fold to make an opening for the head. Use a piece of rope or thin length of fabric as a belt. It's quick and pulls on easily over clothing.

For accessories, shop first at thrift stores, secondhand shops, or garage sales. You can find inexpensive costume jewelry, props, and clothing you can easily adapt.

Keep in mind that for the purposes of your dramas, you need only one definitive prop to establish a character. For instance, while you can put a tunic on several characters, perhaps only the child playing Paul will carry a staff or wear a sash. Maybe only the children playing Roman soldiers or guards will carry cardboard swords. The addition of a few choice props can make all the difference in your production!

So don't fear *simple* costuming such as a staff, a collar, or a piece of purple cloth wrapped around shoulders. Simple isn't bad! The costuming suggestions below assume you have time and resources to turn your dramas into mini-productions.

● Paul

Add a sash to his tunic, or have him wear a bathrobe tunic to set his character apart. Add sandals, a water pouch or gourd, and a walking stick or staff.

● Bible-Times Woman

Wear long skirts, large earrings, and many bracelets. Add a shawl and sandals or go barefoot.

● Roman Soldier or Guard

Use rough cloth to make your tunic, scruff up your hair, and smudge your face with a dark eyebrow pencil or suggest a beard. Even better, recruit a large man in the congregation who already has a beard.

A sword or spear will go a long way in communicating that this is a soldier.

Scenery

Consider giving your four sessions an extra bit of fun by creating a set in the room where you'll have The Depot segments of your program. You could turn a stage or room into a Bible-times road leading to a town, a ship on a stormy sea, or the interior of a prison cell.

If you keep the set general in nature—an outdoor "Bible-times" set—then you can probably use it for your dramas. Or you could create four separate scenes across your stage or on separate walls of your meeting area. The four scenes can depict the four stories about Paul that you'll be studying.

You can create a set by...

● painting on large sheets of paper or lightweight cotton dropcloths to make backdrops, then hanging them on the walls. Or paint backdrops on old bed-sheets, and tape them to the wall or hang them from the ceiling. Two bedsheets attached to the corner of a room create an instant, cozy room set and can be easily put up and taken down.

● creating a Bible-times road by taping lengths of brown packing paper together, then taping them to the floor. Add a few large rocks, or make your own by crumpling brown paper bags and spraying them with gray paint. Place sparse silk greenery here and there along your road as roadside vegetation.

Use large sheets of poster board or cardboard to create a "cityscape" in the background of your road. Just cut rectangles of varying heights, and tape them next to each other along a wall. Use black markers to add the illusion of stones and bricks, and draw in a few windows and doors.

● creating a ship using cut-apart appliance boxes taped end to end. For safety's sake, try to place your boat against a wall rather than have it free-standing. Make a mast by placing a bucket of sand inside your boat, next to the wall. Stick a long dowel from a lumber store into the bucket of sand. Tape a bedsheet sail to the dowel to complete the basic boat. Then drape an old volleyball net over the side of the boat, and add a few ropes for effect. Paint a large sponge black, add a length of chain to it, and hang it over the hull as an anchor.

To create a stormy sea around your boat, cut smaller cardboard boxes into peaks, then paint them blue. Add whitecaps at the tops of the waves by painting the tips of the waves white. To add a three-dimensional effect, paint the tips of the waves white using Spackle or putty.

● making a prison cell by hanging black crepe paper from the ceiling as the bars of the cell. Make paper-loop chains for the prisoners to wear, or, better yet, buy lengths of actual chain from a hardware store. (Kids will love the clinking sound!) Your jailer can wear a chain around his or her waist. Attach a bunch of keys to a large key ring. You can usually find old keys at thrift stores. Loop the chain belt through the key ring before wearing. (There's more of that clinking!)

● creating chariots from large boxes. Add cardboard wheels, and hang ropes over the front of the chariot for use by Roman soldiers.

● attaching twinkling Christmas lights to the ceiling if you'd like to approximate a night scene.

The Depot

For the next four weeks, you'll lead The Depot portion of the BibleVentures program. Each week children will gather at The Depot for an opening time and a closing time. Each segment lasts about ten minutes.

At The Depot, kids sing, review the Venture Verse, and participate in an attention-grabbing experience that introduces the Bible Point. The following lessons will provide all the information you need to have a great time leading this segment of the BibleVenture program!

After the opening, groups of children (Venture Teams) will travel to Venture Centers. Children will stay in the Venture Centers for forty minutes, then return to The Depot for a time of closing and celebration.

During this BibleVenture, children will dig into the life of Paul. Children will discover that God can change their lives, just as God changed Paul. That's an important lesson to learn...and put into action!

You'll see the "God can change you" Bible Point mentioned several times in your lessons. That's intentional: Repetition helps children hear and remember. And by the end of this BibleVenture program, children will have considered the many ways they can be used by God to make a difference in the lives of others!

You've been carefully selected to serve in this role. You have the abilities, attitude, and love of Jesus and kids that it takes to engage and involve children. You'll make good use of those abilities in this program!

Here's a quick outline of your responsibilities as leader of The Depot:

1. Meet and greet kids.

You're the upfront face kids will see each week; it matters how you go out of your way to individually greet as many children as possible. A smile and handshake or pat on the back from you can make a child's day.

Because you'll be making the first impression, it's important you arrive *before* children come. You'll also need to set up and either supervise—or do—the distribution of visas.

2. Oversee visa distribution.

As children arrive at The Depot, they'll stop at the Depot ticket window to sign in, get their name tags, and pick up their BibleVenture Visas. The ticket window can be as simple as a table with a sign on it or as elaborate as a booth with a ticket window cut in it.

For an inexpensive, portable booth, set a refrigerator box on end and cut a door in the back and a ticket window in the front. Prime and paint the booth with bright colors, and you'll have a lightweight booth with room inside for one medium-sized adult.

And while you should oversee this function, it's going to be very difficult for you to staff it and take care of everything else that's happening as you lead the program. There will always be children who come a little late and want to sign in while you're up front leading a song.

So unless you can be two places at once, it's important you recruit a helper. We call that person the "Servant Leader" because he or she serves you and others—and that's true leadership!

You'll find a job description for the role of Servant Leader on page 85.

3. Set up for the opening and closing!

The following lessons will tell you everything you need to know. And though the required supplies are simple and easy to find, it will help if you plan ahead.

Again, your life will be far easier if you recruit a Servant Leader to keep the supply cabinet stocked and the sign in and sign out processes organized.

The Depot

God Can Change You

Venture Verse: "Therefore, if anyone is in Christ, he is a new creation; the old has gone, the new has come!" (2 Corinthians 5:17).

Supplies for Week 1
- Bible
- CD player
- *BibleVentures: Paul* CD
- adult or teen volunteer
- old sheet or dropcloth
- light-colored paint smock
- 2 large paintbrushes
- shallow pan partially filled with brown tempura paint
- paper
- pens
- 1 pad of small sticky notes per Venture Group

The Depot: *Opening*
As children arrive, play "Welcome Music" (track 10) on the *BibleVentures: Paul* CD in the background.  Welcome children and encourage them to sit with others in their Venture Teams. Be sure children know which Venture Team to join and are welcomed warmly.

SAY **It's so exciting to begin our journey together here at The Depot! We'll gather here at the beginning and end of each Bible adventure. Since this is the first week of our adventure, I want to be sure you all know what Venture Team you'll be on for this BibleVenture.**

Have children check their name tags, BibleVenture Visas, or other list you've created so they know what Venture Teams they're on. Ask children to sit with their Venture Teams during The Depot gathering time.

SAY **We're going to spend the next four weeks learning about Paul, a man whose life took a dramatic turn when he met Jesus. Each week you'll have the opportunity to learn something new about Paul as you travel to a different**

Venture view

Establish a nonverbal signal to use to direct kids' attention back to yourself. Suggestion: Clap your hands, flick the lights, blow a wooden train whistle, or use some other unusual sound maker that won't be mistaken in the midst of discussion. Practice the signal several times until kids recognize and respond to it.

Venture Center. And through all our adventures, we'll be reminded that, just as God changed Paul, **(BP)** **God can change *you*!**

In fact, Paul himself said it best right here in the Bible. Hold up your Bible. **Well, actually *God* said it best because he told Paul what to write in 2 Corinthians 5:17! Listen while I read the verse. If you have your Bible with you, follow along.**

Pause briefly to give kids a chance to look up the verse. Then read 2 Corinthians 5:17 aloud: **"Therefore, if anyone is in Christ, he is a new creation; the old has gone, the new has come!"** Have kids repeat the verse with you several times so it sticks with them!

SAY **What a powerful verse! Before Paul came to know Jesus, he worked *against* Christians. In fact, he was so against Christians that he wanted them arrested—even killed. But after he came to believe in Jesus, he changed completely and became one of the most important leaders in the early church.**

Paul became a new creation. When *we* know Jesus, *we* become new creations. That's great news! Hey, there's that word again—*new*. Let's talk for a minute about things that can be new. Think of things in your life that can be new. You can go to a new school or move to a new house. Think of some other things that can be new, and call out your answers to me.

Listen as kids call out answers, and repeat what they say loudly enough for everyone to hear.

SAY **You thought of lots of things that can be new. Thanks! You know, the new things are usually very different from the old things. Your new school is very different from your old one. Your new house isn't anything like your old one. That's one characteristic of something that's new—it's different from something old. Can you think of another characteristic of something new?** Pause.

One thing that comes to my mind is that new things are nice and clean. Let me show you what I mean. I'll need two volunteers.

Choose two volunteers to come forward. Have your adult or teen volunteer come out wearing the smock. Spread an old sheet on the floor, and have all three volunteers stand on it. Give each child volunteer a large paintbrush. Hold the pan with the paint in it yourself.

SAY **During the next few weeks, we're going to discover how God changed Paul and made him new, just like our Bible verse says. We'll also discover that (BP) God can change you, too! Before we know Jesus, our old selves are**

covered with sins. It's like this. We may tell lies. Let one of your child volunteers dip the paintbrush lightly in the paint and brush it on the smock. **We may cheat.** Let the other child paint a stroke on the smock. **We may say mean things about our friends.** Pause for a child to paint. **We may gossip.** Pause for a child to paint. **We may steal.** Pause for a child to paint.

Yuck! Look how dirty and ugly our volunteer's clothes are now, covered with those sins. That's what our old selves are like. And you know what? The only way to get rid of the dirty sins that cover us is to get to know Jesus. When we believe in Jesus, we can become new and clean again. Have your volunteer take off the smock and throw it on the floor. **See? The old is gone, just like the verse says. When we believe in Jesus, God will forgive us for our sins. We become new creations!**

Lead kids in a round of applause as you dismiss your volunteers.

SAY **Let's talk a little more about why we need to be new creations.**

Give each Venture Team a sheet of paper and a pen. Have team members sit in a circle, and ask the BibleVenture Buddy to choose one person to be the Recorder who will write the team's ideas. Explain that Venture Teams will brainstorm lists of sins that kids their age might be tempted to commit. The Recorders will write everyone's answers on the paper. Tell kids to keep going around the circle until no one can think of a new answer. As kids work, play "Food for Thought Music" (track 11) on the CD in the background. 🔘

Encourage kids to examine their hearts as they answer, thinking of things they need to be forgiven for. Tell the Recorders to make sure they write their Venture Teams' names or numbers on the pages. After a few minutes, call time.

SAY **Thanks for making those lists! I'm going to collect these papers, and we'll use them later in our session. In a few minutes, we'll be going to our Venture Centers. But before we do, let's sing a song to help us remember how God can change us.**

🔘 Lead children in singing "Miracles Happen Every Day" (track 1) with the CD. Every time you sing the word "Alleluia," lead children in waving their arms back and forth in the air.

SAY **And now it's time to travel to our Venture Centers!**

Have the leaders of each Venture Center guide the Venture Teams to the area where they'll meet. Children will remain at the Venture Centers for forty minutes. When thirty-five minutes have passed, signal the Venture Center Leaders to let them know it's time to wrap up their activities and move children back to The Depot for the closing.

The lyrics to the songs on your *BibleVentures: Paul* CD are on pages 81-82 of this manual.

If you'd like to extend your time of worship and singing, lead children in singing one or more of the other songs on the *BibleVentures: Paul* CD.

The Depot: *Closing*

 As children begin entering the room, start singing "Miracles Happen Every Day" (track 1) with the CD. Continue singing until all the Venture Teams have returned to The Depot.

SAY **Welcome back to The Depot! I'm sure each of you had an exciting adventure as you learned more about Paul. And as we learn about how God changed Paul, we want to remember that**  **God can change you and me, too! Let's use those lists we made earlier to help us explore how God can change us this week.**

Have each Venture Team stand in a circle. Give each team pens, a pad of small sticky notes, and its list from the opening Depot session. Explain that as the Recorder reads a sin from the team's list, each person in the team should stick a blank sticky note to his or her clothing.

When team members are covered with sticky notes, continue.

SAY **Our old selves are covered with sins. The only way to become new creations is through knowing Jesus. Let's pray together about that.**

PRAY **Dear God, thank you so much for sending Jesus to take away our sins and make us new creations. Help us know, love, and follow Jesus each day this week. In Jesus' name, amen.**

SAY **Carefully take off the sins that cover you, and stick one of them on the page in your visa that shows Paul on the ground. You can throw the rest away on your way out.**

Now think of one particular sin you have trouble with—one area of your life in which you're struggling. Write that sin on the blank space on your visa page, and also write it on the sticky note. Silently ask God to help you change that behavior and make you a new creation.

Give teams a few minutes to take off the sticky notes and write in their visas. Encourage older children to help younger ones who may not be confident in their writing skills. As children write, softly play "Into My Heart" (track 2) on the CD in the background.

When children have finished, have them hold their Venture Visas.

SAY **Remember that God changed Paul and**  **God can change you, too. Take your sticky note home today, and stick it someplace you'll see it often. Maybe you'll stick it on your notebook or bathroom mirror. Every day this week, ask God to change that area of your life and make you a new creation.**

Next week we'll check in together. We'll also discover more about how God changed Paul and 🆒 **God can change you! Have a great week!**

Ask children to leave their Venture Visas (and name tags if you've created permanent ones) at the ticket window as they leave. Play the CD, and let those children still waiting for their parents join you in singing a few more songs of praise.

God Can Change You

Venture Verse: "Therefore, if anyone is in Christ, he is a new creation; the old has gone, the new has come!" (2 Corinthians 5:17).

Supplies for Week 2

- Bible
- CD player
- *BibleVentures: Paul* CD
- fine-tipped colored markers
- shallow pan
- mixing bowl
- metal spoon
- 2 or 3 porous rocks
- 5 or 6 pieces of charcoal
- measuring cup
- newspaper
- ¼ cup of ammonia already measured into a jar with a lid
- ¼ cup of salt
- ¼ cup of liquid bluing (found in the laundry aisle at your grocery store)
- food coloring (any color)
- supplies for the closing activity: plastic jewels, bags, small rocks

The Depot: *Opening*

Before the session, gather the supplies for the experiment on a tray or rolling table for easy transport when it's time to do the experiment. The supplies you'll need include the newspaper, porous rocks, charcoal pieces, measuring cup, ammonia, salt, liquid bluing, food coloring, shallow pan, mixing bowl, and metal spoon.

As children arrive, play "Welcome Music" (track 10) on the CD. Welcome children and encourage them to sit with others in their Venture Teams. Be sure children who were not here last week know which Venture Teams to join and are welcomed warmly.

SAY **Welcome, everyone! We're back to continue our BibleVenture about Paul. As we discovered last week, God changed Paul and**  **God can change you, too! Let's spend just a little time checking in with each other.**

Have kids discuss the following questions in their Venture Teams, led by their BibleVenture Buddies.

ASK

● **How did you see God working in your life last week?**

● **How is God helping you with the area of your life you wrote about in your visa last week?**

After a short time of sharing, call everyone's attention back to you.

SAY **Thanks for sharing your experiences with each other! It's so exciting to know that** **God can change us! Does anyone remember the verse we learned last week about becoming new creations?**

Let volunteers say the verse for the rest of the group. Then lead everyone in repeating 2 Corinthians 5:17 together: "**Therefore, if anyone is in Christ, he is a new creation; the old has gone, the new has come!**"

SAY **Paul was a very unlikely person to become a leader of the faith. As we discovered last week, Paul was out to stop Christians from talking about Jesus. But after he met Jesus, Paul became a new creation. Then he couldn't** *stop* **talking about Jesus!**

In fact, he traveled all over to tell people about Jesus. He wrote lots of letters to the new believers, too. But things weren't always easy for Paul. During his travels he was beaten, thrown in prison, and...Well, why don't I let Paul tell you himself? Listen to what Paul says in one of his letters.

Have a volunteer come forward and read aloud 2 Corinthians 6:3-10 for the rest of the group. Then thank your volunteer and have him or her sit down.

SAY **Paul's life may have gotten rocky, but he was always full of joy because he was a new creation in Christ. Let's do an experiment to show how even a rocky situation can be beautiful! I'll need a few volunteers.**

Choose up to eight volunteers to come forward. Set the supplies you gathered for the experiment on a newspaper-covered table that everyone can see. Have a volunteer hold up the porous rocks.

SAY **Paul's life got kind of rocky as he tried to tell others about Jesus. These rocks can remind us of our own rocky times in life.**

Place the rocks in the shallow pan.

Preselect a capable reader as your volunteer.

You can use fewer than eight volunteers, but the more kids involved, the better!

You may want to put the charcoal pieces in a plastic bag so the volunteer's hands stay clean.

ASK

● **What's one rocky or difficult time you've experienced? Tell your Venture Team about it.**

● **How do you cope during hard times? Who or what helps you?**

Give teams a few minutes to share experiences.  As team members share, play "Rocky Times Music" (track 14) on the CD in the background. Then use your attention-getting signal to regain everyone's attention. Have another volunteer hold up the pieces of charcoal.

SAY **As we heard in Paul's letter, he went through some dark times because of his faith in Jesus. These pieces of charcoal can remind us of dark times we face because of our faith.**

Place the charcoal pieces in the shallow pan with the rocks. Then have kids discuss the following questions in their Venture Teams. If you have time and a small number of children, invite volunteers to share their answers with the rest of the large group.

ASK

● **When have you faced dark or difficult times because of your faith in Jesus?**

● **When is it hard for you to share your faith?**

● **How do you think Paul got through the hard times he faced? What could help you during hard times?**

SAY **These rocks and charcoal aren't very pretty, are they? Rocky and dark times aren't very much fun to go through, either. But we can have joy during hard times, just as Paul did, because faith in Jesus makes us new creations! Watch this!**

Have an *adult* volunteer pour the ammonia into the mixing bowl. Have another volunteer pour the salt into the mixing bowl. Then let another volunteer add the liquid bluing to the mixing bowl. One volunteer can squirt a few drops of food coloring into the bowl, and another can mix the ingredients together. A last volunteer can pour the ingredients of the mixing bowl over the rocks and charcoal pieces in the shallow pan.

SAY **Look what's happening! The mixture of ingredients combined with the charcoal pieces caused a chemical reaction. Now, instead of something dirty and ugly, there's something colorful and beautiful growing!**

That's what it's like when we know Jesus—we become new creations! Just

Make life easy for your BibleVenture Buddies and yourself by making a copy of the questions for each Buddy. Then you won't have to keep interrupting the discussion flow to ask the next question.

Ammonia can be a dangerous substance, so make sure an adult handles it. If kids get any on their skin, wash thoroughly right away. Do this experiment once at home to be sure you know how quickly crystals grow and so you know how many fumes will be released. Do this experiment in a large room where fumes will be safely dispersed.

If you'd like to extend your time of worship and singing, lead children in singing one or more of the other songs on the *BibleVentures: Paul* CD.

as the beautiful crystals are a new creation out of the dark and dirty charcoal, knowing Jesus makes us new creations. God changed Paul into a new creation, and  **BP** **God can change you, too!**

Before we head out to our Venture Centers, let's praise God for changing our lives!

Lead children in singing "I'm Gonna Sing, Sing, Sing" (track 3) with the CD.

After the song,

SAY **As you're at your Venture Center today, think about how God changed Paul into a new creation so that even hard times became joyful. Then trust God to change your life! Right now it's time to travel to our Venture Centers!**

Have BibleVenture Buddies guide the Venture Teams assigned to them to the area where they'll meet. Children will remain at the Venture Centers for forty minutes. When thirty-five minutes have passed, signal the Venture Center Leaders to let them know it's time to wrap up their activities and move children back to The Depot for the closing.

The Depot: *Closing*

Before children arrive, make supply bags for each Venture Team. You'll need two bags for each team. One bag should contain a small rock for each team member. The other bag should contain a small plastic jewel (available at craft shops) for each team member.

As children begin entering the room, start singing "I'm Gonna Sing, Sing, Sing" (track 3) with the CD. Continue singing until all the Venture Teams have returned to The Depot.

SAY **Welcome back to The Depot! I'm sure each of you had an exciting adventure as you learned more about Paul. And as we learn more about how God changed Paul, remember that** **BP** **God can change you and me, too! Let's talk more about how God can change us in the coming week. We'll spend just a little time checking in with each other.**

Ask children to take out their Venture Visas and sit in a circle with their Venture Teams. Give each team a supply of fine-tipped colored markers to share. Ask children to review with their BibleVenture Buddies what they wrote on the inside cover last week. Remind kids that they wrote one sin or area of their lives that they need God's help to change. Have team members discuss the following questions.

ASK

● **How did you see God working in your life last week?**

● **How is God helping you with the sin you wrote about in your visa last week?**

After a short time of sharing, call everyone's attention back to you.

SAY **Thanks for sharing your experiences with each other! It's so exciting to know that BP God can change us! Just as in the experiment we did earlier, God can change even dark and rocky times into something beautiful because we're new creations in Jesus!**

In the blank space on the page in your visa that shows Paul in jail, draw a picture of a rocky time you're facing right now.

Pause long enough to give kids time to draw.

SAY **We all face rocky times in our lives. You may feel like you're the only one, but *everyone* faces hard times. I'd like a volunteer from each Venture Team to come forward to collect something I have to give your team.**

Give each team's volunteer a small bag of rocks. After all volunteers have returned to their teams, continue. Play soft instrumental music during this time ("Instrumental Music for Prayer Time," track 12, is one option).

SAY **Before you pass the bag of rocks around, think of a rocky time someone you know is facing. As you pass the bag of rocks around the circle, I want each person to take a rock and quietly say one word to represent the rocky time the person you know is facing right now. For example, if your friend is having trouble with mean kids at school, you could say "bullies." Or if her dad lost his job, you could just say "work." You may begin.**

Give teams time to pass the rocks. When you see that everyone has a rock, continue.

SAY **Now I'd like another volunteer from each Venture Team to come forward for something else I have for your team.** Give volunteers time to retrieve the bags of jewels and return to their circles. **Now I want you to pass the bag of jewels around the circle. These jewels can remind you that God can change even rocky situations into joyful ones because of the new creations we become in Jesus. As you take a jewel, say a one-sentence prayer, asking God to change the rocky situations we all face into joyful ones. When everyone has prayed, I'll close with a group prayer. Go ahead and begin.**

When you see that everyone has a jewel and teams have finished praying, close with a large-group prayer.

PRAY **Dear God, thank you for hearing us and listening to our prayers. Please be with each person in this room during rocky times. Please be with the people we prayed for. Please comfort and guide all of us during the coming week. Thank you for making us new creations and turning our rocky times into joyful ones because of your Son, Jesus. Help us always remember that you love us. In Jesus' name, amen.**

After you finish praying,

SAY **Take your rocks and jewels home with you this week. Keep them together by your bed or in your backpack where they can remind you that, just as God changed Paul's rocky times into joyful ones, he can do the same for us. You could even give the rock and jewel to the person you prayed for. Tell that person what you learned here—that God changed Paul and  God can change us, too! Have a great week, everyone, and remember that God loves you!**

Play the songs on the CD, and let those children still waiting for their parents join you in singing a few more songs of praise.

The Depot

God Can Change You

Venture Verse: "Therefore, if anyone is in Christ, he is a new creation; the old has gone, the new has come!" (2 Corinthians 5:17).

Supplies for Week 3
● Bible
● CD player
● *BibleVentures: Paul* CD
● 2 white coffee filters per child
● fine-tipped colored markers
● 1 chenille wire per child
● pens

The Depot: *Opening*

Welcome children and encourage them to sit in their Venture Teams. Be sure children who were not here last week know which Venture Teams to join and are welcomed warmly.

SAY **Welcome, everyone! We're back to continue our BibleVenture about Paul. We've been exploring how God changed Paul's life and how** BP **God changes us, too! Let's thank God today with a song!**

Lead children in singing "Jesus Is All the World to Me" (track 4) with the CD.

SAY **As we've been learning, Paul at one time tried to keep Christians from spreading the news about Jesus. But after he became a Christian, Paul told everyone he could about Jesus! Here are a few questions to discuss in your teams.**

ASK

● **Who's the person who first told *you* about Jesus?**

If you'd like to extend your time of worship and singing, lead children in singing one or more of the other songs on the *BibleVentures: Paul* CD.

● Why do you think that person told you about Jesus?

● Why is it important for you to tell others about Jesus?

SAY **Knowing Jesus brings such wonderful changes in our lives; we want to tell everyone we can about him. That's just what Paul did. Listen to what Paul said in one of his letters in the Bible. When he wrote this letter, he was in prison and awaiting trial for telling others about Jesus.**

Ask a volunteer to come forward and read aloud Colossians 3:16-17.

SAY **Wow! Paul was full of joy and love for Jesus, even though he was in prison for telling others about Jesus. God changed Paul from someone who wanted to keep Christians from talking about Jesus to someone who was willing to die for his faith in Jesus. What a huge change! That reminds me of our Venture Verse. Can anyone say it?** Let kids answer.

Our verse is 2 Corinthians 5:17: "Therefore, if anyone is in Christ, he is a new creation; the old has gone, the new has come!" Let's say that together. Lead kids in repeating the verse with you.

God changed Paul completely. Paul became a new creation after meeting Jesus. That's why it's so important to tell others about Jesus—so they can be changed and become new creations too. Let's do some telling right now!

Give each person two white coffee filters, one nestled inside the other. Set out fine-tipped colored markers for kids to share. Show kids how to smooth out their coffee filters into a circle. Remind kids to keep the filters together to provide a stronger writing surface.

SAY **On your coffee filter, carefully write or draw things you know about Jesus. You might write that Jesus died for our sins, or you might draw a cross. You can write all around the edges of the filter, but don't write in the middle. You'll see why in a minute. Write or draw as many things as you can before I call time. You'll have two minutes.**

As kids work, play "Creation Station Music" (track 13) on the CD.  After two minutes, call time.

SAY **Our papers are filled with great information about Jesus! But somehow we have to get that information to others, right? Here's how we'll do it.**

Hearing our Venture Verse again today got me thinking about things that become new creations. And one thing I thought of was a butterfly. A butterfly starts out as a caterpillar but becomes a new creation when it transforms into a beautiful butterfly. Let's turn our papers into new creations—butterflies that will spread the news about Jesus!

Give each person a chenille wire. Demonstrate how to fold the coffee filters, words facing up, back and forth into an accordion fold. Then cinch the middle of the folded filter, and wrap the middle of a chenille wire around the cinched filter. Bring the two ends of the chenille wire to the front to form antennae.

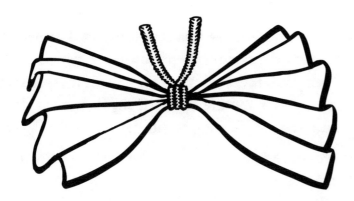

SAY **I'm going to collect these butterflies for now, but you'll see them again in the closing Depot! As you go to your Venture Center today, think about how so many people have learned about Jesus because of Paul's words. Then think of how *you* can tell others about Jesus. Right now, it's time to travel to our Venture Centers!**

Collect the butterflies to use in your closing Depot time. Have the leaders of each Venture Center guide their assigned Venture Teams to the area where they'll meet. Children will remain at the Venture Centers for forty minutes. When thirty-five minutes have passed, signal the Venture Center Leaders to let them know it's time to wrap up their activities and move children back to The Depot for the closing.

The Depot: *Closing*

As children begin entering the room, start singing "Jesus Is All the World to Me" (track 4) with the CD. Continue singing until all the Venture Teams have returned to The Depot.

SAY **Welcome back to The Depot! I'm sure each of you had an exciting adventure as you learned more about Paul and the early church. And as we learn about how God changed Paul, let's remember that (BP) God can change you and me, too!**

ASK

● **In your BibleVenture today, how did you see someone's life change because of hearing about Jesus?** Allow several volunteers to answer.

You don't have to worry about keeping each Venture Team's butterflies separate. Kids won't be receiving their own butterflies in the closing.

If you have a small group, put all the butterflies in a basket and have everyone gather around you. Then toss the butterflies into the air for kids to grab.

If you have a large number of kids, enlist the aid of several BibleVenture Buddies to help you toss the butterflies to kids.

● **How has *your* life changed because of Jesus? Answer that question in your Venture Teams.** Allow several minutes for team members to share answers.

● **Who is one person you can tell about Jesus this week?**

Distribute pens and the Venture Visas to teams.

SAY **On the page of your Venture Visa that shows Paul arriving to tell people about Jesus, write the name of the person you're going to tell about Jesus this week. Then think about exactly what you might say to that person. Let each person on your Venture Team tell one thing he or she might say about Jesus this week.** Ask children to write down what they'll say.

As team members share and write ideas, gather the butterflies kids made in the opening Depot session.

SAY **I have something here that might help you tell others about Jesus. I have the new creation butterflies you made earlier. Remember? They have all kinds of great information written on them about Jesus! OK, here goes!**

Move around the room, tossing butterflies into the air for kids to catch—one butterfly per person.

Explain that after kids each grab a butterfly, they should quickly stand in a circle with their Venture Teams. Tell kids to carefully peek inside the butterflies' wings to read something about Jesus. Have kids go around the circle and each tell one thing about Jesus that they read on their butterflies.

Then have team members face outward in their circles. Count to three, and have kids throw their butterflies into the air for members of other teams to catch. After everyone has picked up a new butterfly, have kids stand in their circles again and share what they read. Then have them face outward and throw those butterflies into the air. In the background, play "Miracles Happen Every Day" (track 1) on the CD.

Repeat for several throws as time allows. Then have children sit on the floor with their Venture Teams. Ask teams to discuss these questions.

ASK

● **Why is it sometimes hard for us to share our faith in Jesus?**

● **After being beaten and thrown in jail, do you think Paul felt like giving up? Would *you* have kept telling people about Jesus? Explain.**

● **What do you think will be the hardest part for you this week as you try to tell others about Jesus?**

SAY **Sometimes it can be scary to tell others about Jesus. But remember, God changed Paul into a new creation, and** 🔵BP **God can change you and me, too! When we're new creations in Christ, God will help us tell others about Jesus. We don't have to be afraid. Here's a song to give us courage!**

🔘 Lead kids in singing "Ho-Ho-Ho-Hosanna" (track 5) with the CD. Every time kids sing the word "Lord," have them "fly" their butterflies back and forth in the air. After the song, lead teams in a closing prayer.

PRAY **Dear Lord, thank you for changing us and making us new creations in Jesus. Help us be bold this week and tell others about Jesus, just as Paul did. Give us courage and the right words to say. Thank you for loving us and for sending Jesus. In Jesus' name, amen.**

Encourage kids to take their butterflies home with them to remind them that, just as God changed Paul into a new creation through Jesus, 🔵BP God can change us, too! Tell kids that their butterflies help them remember what to say this week as they tell others about Jesus.

Ask children to leave their Venture Visas (and name tags if you've created permanent ones) at the ticket window as they leave. Play the CD, and let those children still waiting for their parents join you in singing a few more songs of praise.

The Depot

God Can Change You

Venture Verse: "Therefore, if anyone is in Christ, he is a new creation; the old has gone, the new has come!" (2 Corinthians 5:17).

Supplies for Week 4
- Bible
- CD player
- *BibleVentures: Paul* CD
- pens
- at least 1 plain sugar cookie per child
- paper plates and napkins
- plastic knives
- 1 bowl or container of prepared frosting per Venture Team
- 1 set of decorating supplies, such as small candies, sprinkles, and raisins, per group

The Depot: *Opening*

Welcome children and encourage them to sit with others in their Venture Teams. Be sure children who were not here last week know which Venture Teams to join and are welcomed warmly.

Lead the children in singing "Christ the Solid Rock" (track 6) with the CD.

SAY **It's our last day to learn about Paul here at BibleVentures. For the past few weeks, we've been learning how God changed Paul and made him a new creation. And we've also been learning that** **God can change you and me, too! Remember our Venture Verse? It's 2 Corinthians 5:17. Let's say it together: "Therefore, if anyone is in Christ, he is a new creation; the old has gone, the new has come!"** Lead kids in repeating the verse several times together.

Now let's play a game to help us think about what it means to be a new creation in Jesus.

Have team members form trios. Leaders may need to join in to make sure everyone has two partners for the game. Explain that your game is somewhat

If you'd like to extend your time of worship and singing, lead children in singing one or more of the other songs on the *BibleVentures: Paul* CD.

Explain that unlike Rock, Paper, Scissors, no action is more powerful than another in this game. Our thoughts, words, and actions are all important in God's eyes!

On a large sheet of newsprint, write which action each number represents. Hang the newsprint where everyone can refer to it during the game.

Be sure to call out a different number each time so everyone gets a chance to answer.

If kids seem stuck, it might be helpful to have them think of how someone who doesn't know or obey Jesus might respond to the situation; then they can think, say, or do the opposite!

Feel free to make up your own scenarios too!

similar to Rock, Paper, Scissors but that this game is called Think, Say, or Do. First, tell kids to decide who in each trio will be number one, two, and three. Kids will keep their same numbers throughout the game. Number ones will be the Thinkers, number twos will be the Sayers, and number threes will be the Doers.

Explain that you'll read several situations. After each situation, players will place one hand behind their backs and hold up the number of fingers they've been designated. For example, number ones will hold up one finger, and so on.

When kids are ready, you'll shout, "Think, say, or do!" Kids will hold out their fingers for trio members to see. Then you'll say which number should answer. The child answering should say how he or she could respond to the situation as a new creation in Jesus, depending on which action the number represents.

For example, if you call out number three, the child holding up three fingers will tell what he or she could *do* in that situation as a new creation in Jesus. If you call out number one, the partner holding up one finger will tell what he or she could *think* in that situation as a new creation in Jesus.

When everyone understands the rules, read the following scenarios. Pause after each situation to let trios respond.

Situation 1: You just found out that your friend is having a sleepover Friday night, and you haven't been invited. You see your friend coming toward you in the hall at school.

Situation 2: You and your friends were roughhousing and accidentally broke the arm of the chair that your parents just had reupholstered. Your mom is pulling into the driveway.

Situation 3: You got a D on your math test, and your parents said if you got another bad grade, you'd have to quit soccer. Your dad just asked how your math test went.

Situation 4: You completely forgot that you have a book report due today. You didn't write one, but your friend from another English class has just offered to let you copy hers.

Situation 5: You told your mom that you'd never smoke cigarettes. But the new kid at school who everyone likes just asked if you wanted one. Everyone's looking at you.

Situation 6: The teacher stepped into the hallway for a minute, and everyone's making fun of that quiet girl who just read her essay out loud. The girl was so nervous that she stumbled over words and even mispronounced her own name. You want to fit in with your friends, but you see that she has tears in her eyes.

After the game, have kids regroup with their Venture Teams. Give them several minutes to discuss these questions with their BibleVenture Buddies. As kids discuss, play "Discussion Music" (track 15) on the CD. Make life easy for your BibleVenture Buddies by making copies of the following questions for each Buddy.

ASK

● **Have you ever been in any of the pressure situations I read? What was that like?**

● **How do you decide how to respond to pressure situations in real life?**

● **How can you respond more like a new creation in Jesus during pressure situations?**

● **In our game, all three actions (think, say, and do) were equal; do you think they're equal in real life? Explain.**

SAY **It's important to try to think, say, and do the things Jesus would want us to do. In our game, those three actions were equal. But in real life, all three actions aren't equal. Listen to what the Bible says.** Have a volunteer read aloud James 2:14-17. **See? The Bible says we have to *act* on our faith.**

Let's look back at a couple of those situations I read. It's not enough to *think* about telling the truth or being nice to someone; you have to do it! It's not enough to *say* you'll forgive someone; you have to do it!

And the only way to be able to think, say, and do things that please God is by becoming a new creation in Jesus. God changed Paul, and **BP** **God can change you and me, too! If we believe in Jesus, God will do the rest!**

As you're at your Venture Centers today, think about how God changed Paul. Then be thinking about how **BP** **God can change you and what you would have done in Paul's situation. So let's get going to our Venture Centers! When you come back, I'll have a surprise for you!**

Have the leaders of each Venture Center guide the Venture Teams to the area where they'll meet. Children will remain at the Venture Centers for forty minutes. When thirty-five minutes have passed, signal the Venture Center Leaders to let them know it's time to wrap up their activities and move children back to The Depot for the closing.

The Depot: *Closing*

As children begin entering the room, start singing "Christ the Solid Rock" (track 6) with the CD. Continue singing until all the Venture Teams have returned to The Depot.

SAY **Welcome back to The Depot! I'm sure each of you had an exciting adventure as you learned more about Paul. By now each of you has had a chance to travel to all four of the Venture Centers to learn about Paul and to learn that** (BP) **God can change you!**

Let's get into our Venture Teams to share more about how (BP) **God can change you and me.**

Have children circle up with their BibleVenture Buddies. Distribute pens, and ask kids to turn to the page in their Venture Visas that shows Paul in a storm.

SAY **In this picture, Paul was in a real pressure situation. But he acted on his faith and encouraged others during the storm. In the blank space, write or draw a pressure situation you're facing right now. Then we'll ask God to help us.**

After kids have finished writing, lead them in a prayer.

PRAY **Dear Lord, thank you so much for being with us in our pressure situations. Please help each one of us face the pressure in our lives in ways that will please you. Please change us so we have the courage to live and act out our faith in you. Thanks for loving us and for sending Jesus. In Jesus' name, amen.**

Tell kids that before you bring out the surprise, you'd like them to review their time at BibleVenture. Ask the following questions, and allow a minute for teams to discuss each one. Then have two or three teams share their answers with the larger group before moving on to the next question. In the background, softly play "Discussion Music" (track 15) on the CD.

ASK

● **How has our Venture Verse helped you in your relationship with God?**

● **How did God change Paul?**

● **How did God use Paul?**

● **What's one way God has changed you?**

● **What's one thing you've learned through this BibleVenture that you can tell someone at home or at school?**

As kids are discussing the final question, distribute the cookies and decorating supplies for each Venture Team.

SAY **I thought it would be fun to celebrate all we've learned here at BibleVenture! These plain, boring cookies can represent our lives before we know Jesus. But after we know Jesus,** (BP) **God changes us and makes us new creations. Let's make these cookies new creations too!**

Allergy Alert!

Be aware that some children have food allergies that can be dangerous. Know your children, and consult with parents about allergies their children may have. Also be sure to read food labels carefully as hidden ingredients can cause allergy-related problems.

Give kids several minutes to decorate their cookies. Then lead kids in a short prayer of thanksgiving before they enjoy their treats. Play fun praise music in the background as kids relax and eat. "I'm Gonna Sing, Sing, Sing" (track 3) would be a good choice to play.

After the treat, have kids help clean up. Then lead kids in a final Bible Venture praise and worship session!

SAY **As you leave today, take your Venture Visa with you. This booklet will be a reminder of the travels you've had in this BibleVenture about Paul. And it can remind you that (BP) God can change you! Let's take a minute to thank God for changing us!**

Have children stand and join you in singing any of the songs on the CD. Continue singing and praising God as parents arrive to pick up their children.

Alternate Opening or Closing for The Depot

If one of the activities for the opening or closing in The Depot won't work for your setting or facility, you can substitute this idea...

Invite someone from your church or community to share how God has changed his or her life. Perhaps you can invite a missionary to explain how and why he or she came to serve God in that capacity. Or see if your community has a prison ministry where you can find someone who turned from a life of criminal activity after meeting Jesus.

After your guest shares, remind children that God changed Paul in a dramatic way and (BP) God can change us, too!

Venture Center One:  The Drama Center

God Can Change You

Venture Verse: "Therefore, if anyone is in Christ, he is a new creation; the old has gone, the new has come!" (2 Corinthians 5:17).

Welcome!

You'll be leading the Drama Venture Center for the next four weeks.

One great piece of news is that preparing for the four weeks is easy because you prepare just *one* week's lesson—and present it four times!

Here's how your Venture Center works: Each week children gather at The Depot for a time of opening and adventure. While at The Depot, children will get together in their Venture Teams, and then one group (it could be one Venture Team or several, but each will have an adult leader) will travel to your Venture Center.

This group of children will stay with you for forty minutes, then return to The Depot for a time of closing and celebration.

In the weeks that follow, different groups of children will come to your Venture Center. You'll repeat the same activity all four weeks, each week with a different group of children. This allows you to prepare just once and have four weeks of meaningful interaction with children as you lead them closer to God!

Your Venture Center

During this BibleVenture, children will dig into the life of Paul. Children will learn that, just as God changed Paul, God can change them too.

You'll notice that the Point, "God can change you," is mentioned several times in your lesson. That's by intent, and it's important you reinforce the Point by saying it each time—or even more often. By the end of this BibleVenture, children will have considered how God can change them to make a difference in the lives of others.

In your Venture Center, children will use drama to explore the life of Paul. There's no memorizing lines or turning script pages; children simply listen to

Some children are simply too shy to participate in a drama. If you have a very shy child, encourage him or her to be part of a sound effects crew. Also, if you have a very large class, you could let some of the students be on the sound effects crew as well.

Simple sound effects could include waving a sheet of poster board back and forth as thunder, tapping fingers on a table as rain, and making whooshing sounds for the wind. There are sound effects already on your CD, but adding more sound effects can make things even more fun!

If you'd like, videotape the drama. Kids will love watching themselves when you play it back at a later class. Consider having a BibleVenture party at the end of the four sessions, and play the videos of all four sessions as you celebrate.

Establish a nonverbal signal to use to direct kids' attention back to yourself. Suggestion: Clap your hands, flick the lights, blow a wooden train whistle, or use another unusual sound maker that won't be mistaken in the midst of discussion. Practice the signal several times until kids recognize it and respond to it.

sections of the CD as directed in the lesson and act along with the instructions the narrator gives on the CD. What could be easier than an instant, no-prep drama?

Kids will make simple puppets to use as they act out the roles. Using puppets makes it easier for kids to participate because it takes the spotlight off them and puts it on the puppets! Some of the roles require more action and participation than others, but it's important for *every* child to have an opportunity to participate in a role. The drama isn't terribly long, so if you have time, consider playing it again and letting kids switch roles.

Your enthusiasm for this Venture Center and the drama will be passed on to the children you meet each week. Greet them with excitement, encourage them to join in the drama, and have fun!

Preparation

Before children arrive, gather these supplies:
- Bible
- CD player
- *BibleVentures: Paul* CD
- stamp or small stickers to mark in visas (a ship, if you can find it)
- one 4-foot chenille rope (available at craft shops) per child
- one 3-foot poodle rope per child
- 1 gallon-size plastic bag per child
- 2 sandwich-size plastic bags per child
- colored electrical tape
- transparent tape
- permanent markers
- 1 sheet of 17x22-inch paper per child
- newspaper
- scissors
- newsprint
- marker

The script that matches what you'll hear on the CD is included in this leader guide, beginning on page 59. You will *not* need to provide the script for the children, as there are no parts to read or memorize. The script is provided for your reference only. Listen to the CD before your first meeting so you're familiar with the various roles and action in the drama.

Set up a stage area. This may be one side of the room or an actual stage. Your set can be as simple or as elaborate as you wish. You may wish not to provide any scenery and just let kids' imaginations provide the details. That's fine!

Or you could use these simple ideas to provide a little atmosphere for your production.

● Use masking tape to make the shape of a boat on the floor. Or cut cardboard boxes into lengths, tape the ends together, and set them up in the general shape of a boat. Kids will stand inside the shape during the play.

● Create a backdrop against a wall that kids will stand in front of during the play. Use cardboard as the hull of a boat, tape it to the wall, and then tape a sheet to the ceiling and fan it out to the hull as a sail.

● Bunch a blue tarp around your boat as the water.

● Cut white poster board into spiky waves to add depth to your set.

● Provide empty boxes as cargo for kids to throw overboard during the storm.

Instructions are given here for simple "full-size" puppets that kids will have fun manipulating during the script. If you'd like to make smaller puppets, look for the section titled "Alternate Puppet Ideas."

The Venture Center

Welcome children as they enter your Venture Center. Explain that kids will explore the story of Paul and the shipwreck through a drama and will put on the drama themselves!

SAY **We're going to learn about the life of Paul through an instant drama. Each of you will have the opportunity to participate in this drama. Parts are all easy to follow since there are no lines to read or memorize. You'll hear what you're supposed to do as I play the CD and just do the appropriate actions. It's easy, I promise. Let's get started.**

Oh, wait! I forgot an important bit of information: We have to make some actors first!

Give each child a gallon-size plastic bag, two sandwich-size plastic bags, a four-foot length of chenille rope, a three-foot length of poodle rope, and an 11x17-inch sheet of paper. Set out newspaper, permanent markers, scissors, transparent tape, and colored electrical tape for kids to share.

Write the following character parts on a sheet of newsprint: Paul, Julius, Roman soldiers, sailors, other prisoners. Hang the newsprint on the wall. Call kids' attention to the newsprint.

SAY **For our play, we'll need these characters. You can choose whoever you want your puppet to be, but we need to make sure we have all of these essential characters. Let me know which character you want to create.**

It's intentional that these puppets have no legs. Kids will be so busy trying to control the heads and arms that they won't need any legs to distract them!

Also, in this drama, there are no female roles. That's OK. Remind kids that in a drama, everything is pretend even through they're re-enacting real events from history. Girls can play the part of Paul!

Let kids decide who their puppets will be, but make sure you have all of the characters listed on the newsprint. For this play, it's OK if there's more than one Paul—you just can't have *all* Pauls!

All the puppets will be made in the same way. The differentiating characteristic will be the hats they wear or, in Paul's case, don't wear. Show kids how to make a basic puppet. Make a puppet yourself so kids can follow along. It's also good if you've completed one sample puppet at home to display.

 Play "Ship Ahoy!" (track 16) on the CD in the background as kids work.

Here's how to make a puppet: Stuff a gallon-size plastic bag with newspaper to make the head. Gather the bottom, and tape it shut with electrical tape to form the neck. Use permanent markers to draw your character's face on the bag.

Next, tape the four-foot length of chenille rope to the neck so it hangs down. This will be the body. Then tie the middle of the shorter rope to the body, about six inches below the neck, to form the arms.

Finally, stuff the two sandwich bags with newspaper, gather and tape the open ends, and tape one bag to the end of each arm as a hand. (You can draw hands on the bags if you want to, but it's not necessary.)

Alternate Puppet Ideas

If you don't want to make full-size puppets, consider using one of these alternate ideas:
- Make paper-bag puppets. Decorate the paper bag as a face, insert your hand, and use the fold as a mouth.
- Make cup puppets. Decorate a foam cup as a person, cut two holes in the cup, insert your hand in the cup, and put two fingers through the holes as "arms."
- Make sock puppets. Decorate clean white socks as faces. Add small paper hats and yarn hair.
- Make finger puppets. Cut the fingers from rubber gloves, and decorate each finger as a different character. Add plastic thimble hats.

Now for the hats! The sailors will wear—what else?—sailor hats! Julius and the Roman soldiers will wear the same hats, only turned front to back. Paul and the prisoners won't wear any hats, so kids with those puppets can color hair on their puppets' heads.

You'll find directions in the margin for making a basic hat. Kids can personalize their puppets' hats by drawing medallions, names, pictures, or badges on the hats. They'll tape them to the puppets' heads as illustrated.

1. Fold a horizontal sheet of 17x22-inch paper in half sideways.
2. From the folded edge, fold the corners down to meet in the middle.
3. Fold up a bottom flap in each side. Tuck in the surplus flaps.

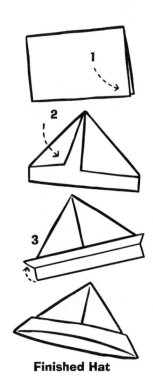

Finished Hat

Gather the children with their puppets. Let kids introduce their characters to each other. Then play "Shipwrecked!" (track 7) on the CD. Tell kids to listen carefully to the narrator, who will guide them in acting out their parts. Encourage kids to have fun and really ham it up as they act out this exciting episode of Paul's life.

After the play, turn off the CD player and have kids use their puppets' hands to give everyone a big round of applause.

SAY **What a great story! This historical event is recorded in the Bible in Acts 27.** Open your Bible to Acts 27, and show kids the chapter. **Tell me what parts of this story you liked best.**

Invite kids to comment on the story. Then have them circle up in their Venture Teams to discuss the following questions with each other and their BibleVenture Buddies.

ASK

● **Have you ever been in a big storm? What was that like?**

● **How would you have felt on that ship? What would you have been thinking?**

● **How do you think Paul felt during that huge storm?**

● **How were Paul's feelings different from the soldiers' feelings?**

● **Why do you think Paul was able to trust God in the middle of such a scary situation?**

● **When are times you have trouble trusting God?**

● **How can Paul's example help you the next time you need to trust God?**

SAY **Our Venture Verse, 2 Corinthians 5:17, reminds us that God will change**

us into new creations when we believe in Jesus. Paul is a perfect example of how God can change a person and use him or her to tell others about Jesus. Paul received great courage from his faith in Jesus. He knew that faith in Jesus is the most important thing in the world, so he never hesitated to tell others about Jesus.

The next time you need courage to share your faith, you have trouble trusting God, or you're in a scary situation, remember Paul. *And* our Venture Verse!

When children finish with their debriefing questions, it should be about time to move back to The Depot. Close your Venture Center with a short prayer, thanking God for giving us the example of Paul and for making us new creations in Jesus. Then help BibleVenture Buddies escort the children back to The Depot for the closing. Kids can take their puppets home with them to remind them that God changed Paul and **(BP)** God can change us, too!

If you still have time....
If you finish before it's time to head back to The Depot, use this activity.

SAY **Our drama was fun, but nothing beats the Bible for excitement. Let's go directly to the Bible to find out the details of this exciting storm story!**

Read Acts 27 aloud. This is an exciting portion of history, so read it with dramatic flair. This is your turn to do the acting! For extra fun, let kids use their puppets to act out the entire chapter.

SAY **God changed Paul to become a new creation. He went from someone who hated Christians to someone who risked his life over and over to tell others about Jesus. (BP) God can change you, too, and use you to spread the good news about Jesus to people in your life!**

This script is provided for your reference. It's recorded on the CD; you don't need to reproduce copies for your kids.

Shipwrecked!

Narrator:

Me, I been a sailin' captain for nigh onto forty year, but I never saw nothin' like that storm what sank us in the Adriatic Sea...

Me and my crew was loadin' the ship—see us workin' there, hauling boxes and jugs aboard? Workin' hard we was when up the gangplank strolls a Roman soldier—a Centurian named Julius—with some prisoners. There's the soldier, standin' all tall and proper-like, and there with his hands chained together is Paul, one of the prisoners.

Well, we set sail, me and my crew working the ropes and the riggin'. The Romans just sat around, and the prisoners couldn't help, on account of being chained up. See the Romans takin' in the sea breeze? And there's Paul, sniffin' the salt air, smilin' like he's enjoyin' the trip. The chains are off now because where's Paul gonna run now that he's out in the ocean?

We stopped at Sidon, then set sail again and put in at Myra. Them names don't mean nothin' to you if you're not a sailor, but mark my word, it was a long trip. And the weather was gettin' rough because it was late in the year.

Paul went to Julius and pointed out at the waves, them gettin' bigger each day. Paul said we should stay put in harbor, where it was safe, for the winter. But Julius and I talked it over, scratchin' our chins and lookin' at the ship. We figured we could make it to Crete, where we'd have a better winter. So I opened the sails, and off we sailed out into open sea.

And that's when it started—the storm of all storms. The wind picked up—not from the south no more but from the *north*—and we started to roll with waves as tall as a man. See how we're leanin' to and fro on the deck? And how us sailors are tryin' to haul in the sails, pullin' as hard as we can? It was a *terrible* storm—and it just got worse...

We were breakin' up—the ship takin' on water—so we tossed all the cargo overboard. See how we're all throwin' stuff into the waves? It's hard to do with the boat rockin' back and forth like that!

Paul spoke up—see him yellin' over the sound of the storm? He said we should have listened to him and that an angel of God told him that all 276 of us on board would live through the storm. But Paul said my ship would run aground and be smashed.

And that's what happened. On the morning of the fifteenth day, we saw an island with a sandy beach. We aimed the ship at the beach, me and my sailors cut loose the anchors, and we raised the sail. The ship was aiming straight at the land...

It never got there. We struck a sandbar, full on, knockin' us all off our feet. The poundin' waves tore apart the back of the boat, so those who could swim—like Paul and the sailors—jumped overboard and made for land.

It was the longest hour of my life, but when we counted up the men on the beach, there were 276 of us standing. No one had died at sea, just like the angel told Paul. 'Twas truly amazing that Paul helped us out even when he was one o' the prisoners!

Aye, and let's give a mighty round of applause to our actors!

Venture Center Two:

God Can Change You

Venture Verse: "Therefore, if anyone is in Christ, he is a new creation; the old has gone, the new has come!" (2 Corinthians 5:17).

Welcome!

You'll be leading the Art Venture Center for the next four weeks.

One great piece of news is that preparing for the four weeks is easy because you prepare just *one* week's lesson —and present it four times!

Here's how your Venture Center works: Each week children gather at The Depot for a time of opening and adventure. While at The Depot, children will get together in their Venture Teams, and then one group (it could be one Venture Team or several, but each will have an adult leader) will travel to your Venture Center.

This group of children will stay with you for forty minutes, then return to The Depot for a time of closing and celebration.

In the weeks that follow, different groups of children will come to your Venture Center. You'll repeat the same activity all four weeks, each week with a different group of children. This allows you to prepare just once and have four weeks of meaningful interaction with children as you lead them closer to God!

Your Venture Center

During this BibleVenture, children will dig into the life of Paul. Children will learn that, just as God changed Paul, God can change them, too.

You'll notice that the Point, "God can change you," is mentioned several times in your lesson. That's by intent, and it's important you reinforce the Point by saying it each time—or even more often. By the end of this BibleVenture, children will have considered the many ways they can be used by God to make a difference in the lives of others.

In your Venture Center, children will use their creative skills to craft a jail. Children will be able to use their projects to retell the Bible story to others.

Your enthusiasm for this Venture Center and the craft will be passed on to the children you meet each week. Greet them with excitement, encourage them to join into the activity, and have fun!

If you have mostly older children in your program, you may choose to have children cut away the back of the boxes themselves.

Preparation

Before children arrive, gather these supplies:

- Bible
- CD player
- *BibleVentures: Paul* CD
- stamp or small stickers to mark in visas
- 1 empty rectangular tissue box with the back cut away per child
- scissors
- glue and tape
- marker and crayons
- 5 or 6 black chenille wires per child
- enough modeling clay for 3 small figures per child

Before children arrive, make a finished jail to show kids.

Place the craft supplies where children will have easy access to them.

Establish a nonverbal signal to use to direct kids' attention back to yourself. Suggestion: Clap your hands, flick the lights, blow a wooden train whistle, or use another unusual sound maker that won't be mistaken in the midst of discussion. Practice the signal several times until kids recognize it and respond to it.

The Venture Center

Welcome children as they enter your Venture Center. Explain that kids will explore the story of how God rescued Paul from prison.

SAY **We're learning how God changed Paul and that**  **God can change you and me! We can read this particular part of Paul's life in Acts 16:16-34.** Open your Bible to Acts 16:16-34, and show kids the passage.

This story is about a time Paul and his friend Silas were put in prison because they were telling people about their faith in Jesus and they helped a slave girl find hope in Jesus. Circle up in your Venture Teams and discuss:

● Why do you think Paul kept talking about Jesus if he knew he could wind up in prison?

● Do you think you would have been as brave as Paul? Why or why not?

Make life easy for your BibleVenture Buddies and yourself by making a copy of the questions for each Buddy. Then you won't have to keep interrupting the discussion flow to ask the next question.

● Is it ever hard for you to share your faith? When and why?

SAY **Paul kept telling others about Jesus, no matter what—even if it meant being thrown in prison. But prison wasn't the end of this story for Paul and his friend.**

Let's listen to a short CD segment to find out what happened. Listen carefully because you'll create an art project that helps you provide action to go with this TV show soundtrack.

You'll hear the soundtrack of a TV show where amazing events are re-enacted. In a few minutes, those events will be re-enacted on a stage you create!

Play "Not-So-Natural Disasters" (track 8) on the CD. A copy of the script on the track is included for your reference (starting on page 65). After the story, stop the CD.

SAY **Wow, what a story! And it really happened, you know. The Bible says so.**

ASK

● **Why do you think Paul and Silas didn't run away after the earthquake?**

● **What happened to the jailer and his family because Paul and Silas stayed put?**

● **Why was it so important for Paul to tell others about Jesus?**

● **How important is it for *you* to tell others about Jesus?**

SAY **Let's make something that will help us tell others about Jesus. We'll make our own prisons so we can tell our families and friends this Bible story. That way, they'll know that God changed Paul and that** BP **God can change us, too!**

Give each child a prepared empty tissue box, five or six black chenille wires, and a lump of modeling clay. Set out glue, tape, scissors, markers, crayons, and other art supplies for kids to share. As kids work, play "Creation Station Music" (track 13) on the CD.

Explain that the interior of the box will be Paul's prison cell. Kids can reach in and draw details of the cell, such as stone walls, benches, and chains on the floor. Demonstrate how to tape the chenille wires to the front opening of the box as prison bars. Have kids use the clay to make three figures—Paul, Silas, and a jailer. From the back opening, have kids carefully set the clay figures inside the cell.

Let kids bend chenille wires to make their figures instead of using clay.

For extra fun, glue small cup hooks to the wall or ceiling of the cell. Attach short lengths of fine chain, available at hardware stores, to the hooks as the prisoners' chains.

Be sure children put their names on their projects.

As children work, move about the room, helping them and talking about the story of Paul's prison escape. Encourage children to share about times they've experienced God's strength and protection.

When everyone has finished making a prison cell, play "Not-So-Natural Disasters" (track 8) on the CD again for the kids. Let kids use their crafts to act out the story along with the CD. Encourage kids to shake their boxes during the earthquake and bend open the chenille-wire prison bars when the story says the prison doors flew open.

After the story, stop the CD and gather everyone.

SAY **That was some great acting! You can take your art projects home with you today. Use them to tell your families and friends the story of how Paul told others about Jesus, even in prison. Remember to tell them that God changed Paul and that** BP **God can change us, too!**

Let's thank God for changing our lives when we meet Jesus!

PRAY **Dear Lord, thank you so much for Jesus. Thank you for changing our lives when we meet him. Help us tell others about Jesus, just as Paul did. We love you. In Jesus' name, amen.**

Have children set aside their projects and take out their Venture Visas.

Place a stamp or sticker on each child's page to signify that he or she has traveled to your Venture Center.

It should be about time to move back to The Depot. Escort the children back to The Depot for the closing.

If you still have time....

If you finish before it's time to head back to The Depot, use the following activity.

Remind kids that even when they were in prison, Paul and Silas sang praise songs to God. So be like Paul and his friends! Lead kids in singing any song from the CD. Let kids make up actions for the song too!

Not-So-Natural Disasters

Narrator:

Welcome, viewers! So glad you could join us today for "Not-So-Natural Disasters." I'm Skippy Skipstone, and on this show, we check out amazing and unexplainable events!

Today we're going to explore what happened in the Bible in Acts 16. I have a cast of actors to re-enact the story.

Two men, followers of Jesus named Paul and Silas, were telling people about Jesus. Paul, Silas, wave to us, guys. Thanks!

Paul and Silas healed a girl who was a slave, and her owners weren't happy about this. So they had Paul and Silas severely beaten and thrown in jail. You can see the walls of the jail there on the stage.

The jailer—nod to us, jailer—was ordered to guard Paul and Silas carefully. So the jailer put Paul and Silas in a jail cell and put their feet into stocks—which means he locked up their feet so they couldn't walk around. Then the jailer left the cell, went home, and went to sleep.

Paul and Silas were sitting in jail, unable to move their feet, waiting to see what would happen to them. They hadn't done anything wrong, but they'd been treated terribly! See them rubbing their aching bodies? They must have been very, very sore from the beating. What do you think they did? Did they cry? No. Complain? No. Believe it or not, they started singing!

Paul and Silas kept on praying and singing to God. The other prisoners were listening to them. At about midnight, there was a sudden earthquake!

Paul and Silas began to shake. The earthquake was so violent that the walls and foundations of the jail were shaken! All the prison doors flew open!

The jailer woke up. He jumped out of bed and ran to the prison.

When he saw the doors open, he assumed the prisoners were gone and drew his sword to kill himself. He knew he'd be punished for letting prisoners

escape. But Paul shouted, "Don't harm yourself! We're all here!" You see, none of the prisoners had left!

The jailer fell on the ground in front of Paul and Silas. He trembled. He asked them, "What must I do to be saved?"

Paul and Silas put their hands on his shoulders and replied, "Believe in the Lord Jesus, and you will be saved."

The jailer did believe. See him smiling and hugging Paul and Silas? He fed them and washed their wounds, and his whole family believed in Jesus! Now isn't that amazing? They all said "yes" to Jesus!

In case you're wondering, Paul and Silas were released the next day and went back to telling others about Jesus.

There you have it, viewers. A "Not-So-Natural Disaster" that changed the lives of many people! I'm Skippy Skipstone saying farewell for now!

Venture Center Three:

God Can Change You

Venture Verse: "Therefore, if anyone is in Christ, he is a new creation; the old has gone, the new has come!" (2 Corinthians 5:17).

Welcome!

You'll be leading the Games Venture Center for the next four weeks.

One great piece of news is that preparing for the four weeks is easy because you prepare just *one* week's lesson—and present it four times!

Here's how your Venture Center works: Each week children gather at The Depot for a time of opening and adventure. While at The Depot, children will get together in their Venture Teams, and then one group (it could be one Venture Team or several, but each will have an adult leader) will travel to your Venture Center.

This group of children will stay with you for forty minutes, then return to The Depot for a time of closing and celebration.

In the weeks that follow, different groups of children will come to your Venture Center. You'll repeat the same activity all four weeks, each week with a different group of children. This allows you to prepare just once and have four weeks of meaningful interaction with children as you lead them closer to God!

Your Venture Center

During this BibleVenture, children will dig into the life of Paul. Children will learn that, just as God changed Paul, God can change them, too.

In your Venture Center, children will use games to explore Paul's missionary journeys. Children *love* to play games, but too often game time is also when kids discover that they're not fast enough, not tall enough, and not as coordinated as everyone else. And anyone who has been picked last for a softball game knows how humiliation feels.

That's why your role in leading this Venture Center is so important. You'll make sure that game time is positive, that everybody plays, that everybody cooperates, and that nobody goes home feeling like a loser.

These games were written *specifically* to help children explore the Bible story accounts. When you use these activities, game time becomes learning time, too!

If you have a small group of kids, you could let them help blow up the balloons, but be aware that this is difficult for many children and unsafe for younger elementary children. Safety first!

If you're playing outdoors, use ropes placed in the grass to mark the playing areas as described here.

Establish a nonverbal signal to use to direct kids' attention back to yourself. Suggestion: Clap your hands, flick the lights, blow a wooden train whistle, or use another unusual sound maker that won't be mistaken in the midst of discussion. Practice the signal several times until kids recognize it and respond to it.

The goal is for kids to play *with* one another, not *against* one another. It's a new concept for some children—and adults, too.

Your enthusiasm for this Venture Center and the games will be passed on to the children you meet each week. Greet them with excitement, encourage them to join in the games, and have fun!

Preparation

Before children arrive, gather these supplies:

● Bible
● CD player
● *BibleVentures: Paul* CD
● stamp or small stickers to mark in visas (footprints or balloons, if you can find them)
● masking tape
● at least 1 balloon per child, plus extras
● trash bag
● markers
● construction paper
● paper plates
● cold water or juice in cups

Prepare your playing area by marking start and finish lines on the floor with masking tape. Hang a sheet of construction paper on the wall in one corner of your room. Blow up and tie off a bunch of balloons, at least one balloon per child, plus a few extra in case of blowouts. Place the balloons in a trash bag until you need them.

For safety's sake, make sure to clear the room of furniture and any other obstacles.

The Venture Center

SAY **We can read in the Bible about many of Paul's missionary journeys. Paul traveled by land and by sea to spread the gospel of Jesus. As you recall, Paul started out as an enemy of the Christians. But then God changed Paul and made him a new creation. Paul spent the rest of his life telling others about Jesus. As we play these games, remember that** **BP** **God can change you and me, too!**

At this Venture Center, we're going to play a few games that will give us a tiny idea of what Paul's life as a missionary might have been like.

The Great Escape

SAY **Right from the start, Paul's life as a Christian was dangerous. Not long after Paul began telling people about Jesus, the Jews in Damascus plotted to kill Paul. Acts 9:19-25 tells what happened.** Have a volunteer read the passage aloud.

What a great escape! Let's play a quick game to see what that night might have been like. Hmm...but we don't have any baskets. That's OK—I have an idea!

Have kids form trios, and have trios stand at the starting line. Explain that the smallest person in each trio will be "Paul" and the other two players will form the basket. Show the basket makers how to cross their arms and hold hands with each other to form a "basket" for Paul to sit in.

Say that when you give the starting signal, trios should travel to the opposite side of the room and back. But since Paul had to escape in the basket at night, you're going to turn off the lights. And since Paul and his friends had to be very quiet so they wouldn't be captured, the basket holders have to tiptoe and the Pauls have to say "Shhhhh!" during the whole game.

Explain that since this isn't a race, trios don't have to compete against each other or even against the clock. Rather, they'll be competing against noise. That is, the goal is to travel as quietly as possible so they aren't easy to detect.

During the game, play "Great Escape Music" (track 17) on the CD.

Give the signal and let trios begin. As trios navigate the room, the soundtrack will mask all but the heaviest footsteps. Occasionally call out, "Where are you?" and "Paul, we're coming to get you!"

A variation of this game is to leave the lights on and compete against the clocks. If you choose to play in this way, use a stopwatch to time the trios. If you have time, let trios play again, trying to beat their previous times. Then have kids sit in their trios to answer the following questions. After each question, invite volunteers to share their answers with the rest of the large group.

ASK

● **What do you think Paul was thinking to himself as his friends helped him escape in the basket?**

● **Why do you think Paul's friends risked helping him?**

● **What would you have done in Paul's place? in his friends' place?**

● **After someone tried to kill you for talking about Jesus, do you think you'd keep talking about him? Why or why not?**

SAY **Let's go back to the Bible to see what other kinds of adventures Paul had as he spread the good news about Jesus.**

Obstacle Course

SAY **Well, Paul didn't let a little murder plot stop him. He kept talking about Jesus wherever he went. And, boy, did he go a lot of places! He walked, and he sailed, and he walked some more. Walking and talking, walking and talking, with some sailing in between. And everywhere he went, he had the same routine.**

When he arrived in a town, he went first to the synagogue (that's where the Jews went to worship) to preach about Jesus to the Jews. Then he preached to the Gentiles. Sometime the people listened, and sometimes they didn't.

Let's say that this corner of the room is the synagogue. Point to the sheet of paper you hung on the wall. **In the rest of our games, remember that no matter what instructions I give you, you have to run and touch the paper synagogue first, OK? OK.**

Paul ran into lots of obstacles as he preached about Jesus. Listen to what the Bible says in Acts 14:1-7. Have a volunteer read the passage aloud for the rest of the large group. **Let's see what it's like to face lots of obstacles.**

Have about five or six kids stand at various spots around the room between the start and finish lines. These kids will be the Obstacles. Give each Obstacle a paper plate. Have the rest of the kids form two lines at the start line. Have balloons ready to give each child in line. During the game, play "Obstacle Course Music" (track 18) on the CD.

SAY **Paul often traveled with fellow believers. In the passage we just heard, he was traveling with a friend named Barnabas. So in this game, players will travel in twos. Pairs will try to bat their balloons, which represent the good news about Jesus, from one side of the room to the other, while weaving in and out of the Obstacles. The Obstacles will wave their paper plates and try to prevent the balloons from getting across the room. Ready? Let's play!**

Give the first players in each line a balloon, then say, "Go!" As the two players begin to bat their balloons, call time immediately.

SAY **Wait a minute, wait a minute! What did you forget?** See if anyone remembers that they were supposed to run to the "synagogue" first. Have kids

Make life easy for your BibleVenture Buddies and yourself by making a copy of the questions for each Buddy. Then you won't have to keep interrupting the discussion flow to ask the next question.

Have a volunteer demonstrate each event as you explain it.

come back to the starting line and begin the game again. Have players run to the corner of the room and touch the paper synagogue, then run back to the starting line and begin play.

Encourage kids in line to cheer for each pair as they try to get their balloons across the room. As each pair reaches the finish line, give the next two players their balloons. Call time whenever anyone forgets to run to the synagogue.

After all pairs have reached the finish line, play again if you have time, letting new players become the Obstacles. Then have kids circle up in their Venture Teams to answer these questions.

ASK

● **What was it like when the Obstacles wouldn't let your balloons get through?**

● **What was it like to try to keep the balloons from crossing the room?**

● **Why do you think some people didn't want to hear the good news about Jesus?**

● **How do you think Paul felt when he heard about another plot to kill him?**

● **If you had been Paul, do you think you would have given up at this point? Explain.**

SAY **Well, Paul still didn't give up. Let's take a little breather while we find out more!**

Keepin' On

SAY **I don't want you to think that all Paul had was trouble! God was with Paul on his journeys, guiding him and protecting him. And lots of people believed in Jesus because of Paul. Let's listen to a quick story about a time the Holy Spirit told Paul where he should travel next and what happened when he got there. Relax, there's no acting this time—we'll just listen! We'll enjoy a nice cold drink while we do!**

Distribute cold water or juice. Then play "Paul's Vision" (track 9) on the CD. It's a short script about the time the Holy Spirit called Paul to preach in Macedonia. Kids will simply listen to the segment as they rest from their games. After the segment, turn off the CD player.

SAY **Paul never gave up, even when he faced obstacles. He was plotted against, beaten, and even thrown in jail. But he kept right on telling**

For extra fun during the triathlon, designate another corner of your room as the jail. Every so often during the games, call time and send the current play to jail for thirty seconds. Explain that Paul was jailed several times for telling others about Jesus.

people about Jesus. It was like he was in a marathon! Let's have a marathon of our own and see if we can keep going like Paul did. In fact, let's have a triathlon—that means there will be three events in the next game! Are you up to the challenge?

Say that the three events in the triathlon will be balloon relays to represent spreading the news about Jesus. Tell kids that you'll explain all three events before beginning.

SAY **The first event will be the Walk the Talk Challenge. Paul had to keep going, even when he was tired and even when it was slow going.**

Have kids form two lines facing each other on opposite sides of the room. With feet close together at the starting line, the first player will place a balloon on the top of his or her feet. The goal is to shuffle to the opposite line while keeping the balloon balanced on top of the feet. Then the first player in the next line will shuffle back across the line, and so on.

SAY **The second event will be the Talk the Talk Challenge. Paul kept talking about Jesus, no matter what. People tried to make him stop talking, but he never ran out of breath when he was talking about Jesus!**

Kids will stay in the same opposite lines. Give each player his or her own balloon to use. The first player will kneel and move the balloon to the opposite line by blowing on it—no hands allowed. The first player in the next line will do the same with his or her balloon, and so on until everyone has blown a balloon across the room.

SAY **The last event in our triathlon is the Don't Get Crabby Crab Walk. Paul may have gotten discouraged at times, but he never got crabby and gave up.**

The first player in line will face backward in a crab walk stance. Balance a balloon on the player's tummy, and let the player crab walk backward to the other line. Then the first player in that line will do the same, and so on until everyone has had a turn.

Have kids form the two lines, and begin the first event. Make sure to call time if anyone forgets to run to the synagogue before playing. This should make for some zaniness during the events.

Encourage kids waiting their turns to cheer on their fellow players during each event.  Play "Walk the Talk" (track 20) on the CD as kids play in the first event. Play "Talk the Talk" (track 21) during the second event. Play "Don't Get Crabby" (track 22) as kids finish up with the third event.

After kids have finished the triathlon, lead them in a round of applause for everyone's participation. Then let kids sit down in their Venture Teams to rest!

SAY **Paul never gave up, no matter what hardships he faced. Want to know why? His answer's right in the Bible! Let's listen to his own words.**

Have a volunteer read aloud Acts 20:22-24.

SAY **That's pretty incredible. He was *really* dedicated to Jesus and to telling everyone he could about Jesus. It's even more amazing when you remember how Paul started out—as a hater of Christians. God sure changed Paul, and**  **God can change you and me, too!**

Remember what our Venture Verse says? Let's say 2 Corinthians 5:17 together: "Therefore, if anyone is in Christ, he is a new creation; the old has gone, the new has come!"

In their Venture Teams, have kids discuss:

● **How do you think Paul was able to keep going with all the hardships he faced?**

● **Have you ever faced a hardship because you're a Christian? Tell your group about it.**

● **When is it hard for you to share your faith? Why?**

● **What might happen if you share your faith, even when it's hard?**

● **What might happen if you don't share your faith?**

SAY **Before we close today, let's do a little demonstration about sharing our faith.**

Have everyone write his or her name on a balloon. Have kids stand in a line that stretches across the room, and have all the balloons at one end of the line. Have kids start passing the balloons slowly from child to child, from one end of the room to the other. When about half of the balloons are in circulation, call time. Let kids finish passing the balloons that are already in progress, but don't let them start any more balloons down the line. Collect the balloons that have been passed, and have kids sit in their teams again.

SAY **Let's say that these balloons represent people who have been told about Jesus. That means that** [child's name from one of the balloons] **has been told about Jesus. And so has** [child's name] **and** [child's name]. Read the names from the balloons that were passed, and hand the balloons to their owners.

I guess that means the rest of you haven't been told about Jesus. Sorry. Pause as kids take this in.

ASK

- ● **How does it feel to be left out of hearing about Jesus?**

- ● **What can you do to keep this from happening to someone else?**

SAY **This was just a demonstration, but it could really happen. If Paul had given up, we may have never heard about Jesus. If *you* give up, someone in your school or your neighborhood might never know about Jesus. Hand out the rest of the balloons to their owners. We have a responsibility to tell others about Jesus. Let's never give up! Let's rely on God to help us. He will, you know. Let's pray.**

PRAY **Dear Lord, thank you for sending Jesus to save us from our sins. Thank you for the courage of the first apostles, who started spreading the gospel to the rest of the world. Help us be like them, to be brave and strong as we tell others about you. In Jesus' name, amen.**

Bring out kids' Venture Visas, and place a sticker on each to show kids have visited your Games Venture Center.

After that, it should be about time to move back to The Depot. Escort the children back to The Depot for the closing.

If you still have time....

If you finish before it's time to head back to The Depot, use the following activity.

Have kids scatter around the room. As with the other games you've played, explain that the balloon in this game represents the good news of Jesus. The object of the game is to keep spreading the good news! Have kids bop the balloon from player to player. As players each bop the balloon, have them call out one thing they could tell others about Jesus. If you have a large group, start several balloons bopping. Soon you'll have the good news bopping all over the room!

Venture Center Four:

God Can Change You

Venture Verse: "Therefore, if anyone is in Christ, he is a new creation; the old has gone, the new has come!" (2 Corinthians 5:17).

Welcome!

You'll be leading the Visual Venture Center for the next four weeks.

One great piece of news is that preparing for the four weeks is easy because you prepare just *one* week's lesson—and present it four times!

Here's how your Venture Center works: Each week children gather at The Depot for a time of opening and adventure. While at The Depot, children will get together in their Venture Teams, and then one group (it could be one Venture Team or several, but each will have an adult leader) will travel to your Venture Center.

This group of children will stay with you for forty minutes and then return to The Depot for a time of closing and celebration.

In the weeks that follow, different groups of children will come to your Venture Center. You'll repeat the same activity all four weeks, each week for a different group of children. This allows you to prepare just once and have four weeks of meaningful interaction with children as you lead them closer to God!

Your Venture Center

During this BibleVenture, children will dig into the life of Paul. Children will learn that, just as God changed Paul, God can change them, too.

You'll notice that the Point, "God can change you," is mentioned several times in your lesson. That's by intent, and it's important that you reinforce the Point by saying it each time—or even more often. By the end of this BibleVenture, children will have considered the many ways they can be used by God to make a difference in the lives of others.

In your Venture Center, children will have the opportunity to learn visually—to explore the account of Paul's conversion in ways that delight visual learners. Children will also dig into the Venture Verse, 2 Corinthians 5:17.

Establish a nonverbal signal to use to direct kids' attention back to yourself. Suggestion: Clap your hands, flick the lights, blow a wooden train whistle, or use another unusual sound maker that won't be mistaken in the midst of discussion. Practice the signal several times until kids recognize it and respond to it.

Preparation

Before children arrive, gather these supplies:

- Bibles
- CD player
- *BibleVentures: Paul* CD
- stamp or small stickers to mark in visas (sunglasses if you can find it)
- at least 4 general interest magazines per group
- paper
- pens
- stack of sticky notes for each group
- VCR and TV
- copy of the movie *A Christmas Carol* (rated PG, 1984, starring George C. Scott)
- pillows
- popcorn
- 1 sheet of poster board per group
- markers, crayons, paint pens, and other art supplies

The Venture Center

In your Venture Center, kids will explore part of Paul's life through visual aids such as magazines, movie clips, and posters.

Bring out the magazines you gathered before class. Turn to a full-page advertisement, and hold it up for everyone to see.

SAY **Look at this advertisement. What do you think the goal of this ad is?** Let kids respond.

Obviously, the main goal of any ad is to get you to buy the product. But how do advertisers *do* that? By trying to convince you that you *need* their product. They try to convince you that if you'll just buy their product, your life will change for the better in some way. And they don't use just words; they use pictures, too. Let's explore that a little more.

Give each team paper, a pen, a stack of sticky notes, and several magazines to look through. Tell each team to appoint a Recorder who will write down the team's ideas. Have teams go through their magazines and flag advertisements that try to convince buyers that their lives will change as a result of the product. For example, an ad might be for shampoo and might show a picture of a girl laughing, surrounded by other happy people. Therefore, the team might say that the picture indicates that if you use that shampoo, you'll be happy and have lots of friends...*plus* clean hair!

Before children arrive, cue the video to the spot where Scrooge gives his "humbug" speech while discussing Christmas with his nephew. This is approximately four minutes into the movie.

The edition of *A Christmas Carol* (PG) that we've chosen is the 1984 version starring George C. Scott as Scrooge. But you can use any version you like—just find the scenes described.

Choose an advertisement to use as an example of what you want kids to look for. Typically, shampoo ads provide good examples because they show the product in use and a happy consumer.

Ask the Recorders to write what their teams think of each ad. Then have each team go back through the flagged pages and choose one advertisement to silently act out for the rest of the large group. The rest of the group will try to guess the product being advertised and the change the product might produce. As teams prepare, play "Advertisements" (track 19) on the CD.  After a few minutes, ask teams to present the advertisements they chose.

After each team's presentation, lead everyone in a round of applause.

SAY **Thanks for your participation! Those advertisement Charades were fun. And they gave us a little insight into how manufacturers try to convert, or change, us.**

But you know, how we change on the outside isn't important. The clothes we wear, the kind of shampoo we use—none of that matters. It's the way we change on the *inside* that counts!

In a little while, we'll talk about how the Master Manufacturer, God, might want to change us!

Right now, let's watch part of a movie about a guy who *really* changed—on the inside, where it counts. But first, let's get comfortable!

Provide pillows for kids to lounge on and popcorn to munch as they watch excerpts from the movie *A Christmas Carol*. To show kids Scrooge before the big change, start showing the movie at approximately 4:00 (four minutes into the movie). This clip shows a conversation between Scrooge and his nephew. The nephew has come to invite Uncle Scrooge to Christmas dinner. Scrooge dismisses Christmas with a "humbuggy" diatribe all his own. The scene will demonstrate what a mean, disagreeable person Scrooge once was. Stop the movie at approximately 4:50.

Have kids discuss these questions in their teams:

- **What do you think of our main character, Scrooge?**

- **How do you think other people feel about him?**

- **Do you think Scrooge is happy? Why or why not?**

SAY **Scrooge doesn't seem like a very nice guy, does he? Let's find out what happens to him.**

As teams talk, fast-forward the movie to approximately 1:25:40. The scene you want shows Scrooge on Christmas morning and demonstrates how he changed after his eye-opening experience! Play the scene, stopping the movie at approximately 1:27:30.

Make life easy for your BibleVenture Buddies and yourself by making a copy of the questions for each Buddy. Then you won't have to keep interrupting the discussion flow to ask the next question.

If you have mostly young children on your teams, ask the BibleVenture Buddies to read the story aloud. You could also paraphrase the story or read it from a children's story Bible.

Have kids discuss these questions in their teams:

● **How did Scrooge change?**

● **Why do you think he changed?**

● **Do you think he was happier before or after the change? Explain.**

● **How did the change affect other people?**

SAY **There's no doubt that Scrooge underwent a *major* change—for the better! But this was just a movie. I want to tell you about someone who underwent a major change for the better in real life!**

For a great example of how God can change someone, we can look at Paul. God changed Paul, and  **God can change you, too!**

Paul was walking along the road to Damascus one day, just minding his own business. Well, sort of. Actually, he was out to nab some more Christians! You see, Paul *hated* Christians. He thought they were wrong about Jesus and that they were hurting the Jewish faith. But then something incredible happened. I'll let you find out what it was!

Give each team a Bible, and have kids open to Acts 9.

SAY **In your team, take turns reading aloud Acts 9 to see what happened to Paul. Oh, and I should tell you something—his name was Saul at the time this story took place. His name changed to Paul a little later. When your team has finished reading, raise your hands.**

When everyone has finished reading, use your attention-getting signal. Have kids answer the following questions in their teams. After each question, invite volunteers to share their team's insights with the rest of the large group.

● **What happened to Paul?**

● **How did Paul change as a result of coming in contact with Jesus?**

● **How has knowing Jesus changed *your* life?**

SAY **Before Paul met Jesus, he didn't believe Jesus was God's Son. In fact, he wanted to stop Christians in their tracks. But after he met Jesus, his whole life changed! He became a new creation, just like our Venture Verse says. Let's say our verse together.**

Lead kids in reading or repeating 2 Corinthians 5:17 with you: **"Therefore, if anyone is in Christ, he is a new creation; the old has gone, the new has come!"**

If you have mostly older kids in class, let each child make an individual poster. The poster should depict personal changes kids have experienced as a result of knowing Jesus, as well as changes they'd like God to make in them as they grow.

After the first week of this BibleVenture, children in your Venture Center will know more details about the life of Paul. Encourage children to share what they've learned about Paul's life so far.

Wow! That verse was sure true for Paul! And it can be true for us, too. BP God can change you, and then he can use you to tell others about Jesus, just as he did with Paul.

Give each team a sheet of poster board, markers, crayons, and other art supplies.

SAY **As a team, I want you to make an advertisement for becoming a Christian. Think about how knowing Jesus changed Paul's life and how it has changed your life. Then make a poster that would attract others to Christianity. Make sure everyone on your team contributes to the poster. You'll have five minutes. Ready? Go!**

As kids are working, softly play any of the songs from the *BibleVenture: Paul* CD.

Wander the room, offering help as needed. Encourage older kids to help younger ones contribute to the poster. Also encourage kids to use their Bibles to look up verses they may want to include on their posters.

After five minutes, call time. Let each team present its poster to the rest of the large group. After each presentation, lead kids in a round of applause.

SAY **Thanks for those posters! We can all influence others for Jesus. We may not have to make posters for them, but we can influence them in other ways. The way we act, the way we talk, how we treat other people—those are all ways to show that we're Christians and to introduce other people to Jesus.**

Let's pray that God will change us, just as he changed Paul, and that he'll use us to tell others about Jesus, as Paul did.

PRAY **Dear Lord, thank you for Jesus. Thank you for the changes he makes in our lives. Help us be like Paul and tell others about Jesus every chance we get. Give us the courage to do that, please. In Jesus' name, amen.**

After discussing the posters, it should be about time to move back to The Depot. Have children take out their Venture Visas and open to the page that shows Paul kneeling in the road. Place a stamp or sticker in the space provided to show that kids have visited your Venture Center.

Close your Venture Center with a short prayer, thanking God for giving us the example of Paul and for using us today. Then escort the children back to The Depot for the closing.

If you still have time....

If you finish before it's time to head back to The Depot, use the following activity.

Have children join you in singing "Miracles Happen Every Day" (track 1) with the CD.  Encourage children to work together to make up motions to express the lyrics of the song. Play the song several times, letting children clap and do the motions they've created.

Song Lyrics

Miracles Happen Every Day

Miracles happen when we pray. Alleluia!

Miracles happen every day. Alleluia!

God is great and powerful. Alleluia!

And he still works miracles. Alleluia!

Let's praise God, everyone, Alleluia!

For the miracles he's done. Alleluia!

Into My Heart

Into my heart, into my heart,

Come into my heart, Lord Jesus.

Come in today; come in to stay;

Come into my heart, Lord Jesus.

Come in today; come in to stay;

Come into my heart, Lord Jesus.

I'm Gonna Sing, Sing, Sing

I'm gonna sing, sing, sing.

I'm gonna shout, shout, shout.

I'm gonna sing, I'm gonna shout:
Praise the Lord!

When those gates swing open wide,

I'll be sittin' by Jesus' side.

I'm gonna sing, I'm gonna shout:
Praise the Lord!

I'm gonna sing, I'm gonna shout:
Praise the Lord!

Song Lyrics

Jesus Is All the World to Me

Jesus is all the world to me:

My life, my joy, my all.

He is my strength from day to day;

Without him I would fall.

When I am sad, to him I go.

No other one can cheer me so.

When I am sad,

He makes me glad;

He's my friend.

Ho-Ho-Ho-Hosanna

Ho-ho-ho-ho-sanna!

Ha-ha-la-le-lujah!

He he he he saved me.

I've got the joy of the Lord!

Ho-ho-ho-ho-sanna!

Ha-ha-la-le-lujah!

He he he he saved me.

I've got the joy of the Lord!

Christ the Solid Rock

My hope is built on nothing less

Than Jesus' blood and righteousness;

I dare not trust the sweetest frame

But wholly lean on Jesus' name.

On Christ, the solid rock, I stand—

All other ground is sinking sand;

All other ground is sinking sand.

When he shall come with trumpet sound,

Oh, may I then in him be found,

Dressed in his righteousness alone,

Faultless to stand before the throne.

Job Description: BibleVenture Buddy

BibleVenture Buddies have the joy—and the challenge—of connecting with kids in a deep, significant way.

As a BibleVenture Buddy, here's what you'll become to the kids in your care...

A trusted friend. You're a grown-up who's glad these kids came, who knows their names, who's been praying about what's important to them. Your focused attention and listening ear help your kids realize they're important to you—and to God.

A role model. How you interact with kids sets the tone for how they'll interact with each other.

A guide. Instead of being the "teacher" with all the answers, you're someone who asks great questions. You jump in and enthusiastically do the activities *they* do at BibleVenture. You gently guide kids as they discover how to apply God's Word to their lives and enter into a deeper relationship with Jesus.

A steady influence in kids' lives. From week to week, you're there with a smile and kind word. You don't demand that kids perform to earn your approval. You don't give kids grades. You're in their corner, dependably cheering them on.

And as you serve God and the kids in your Venture Team, you'll help Jesus touch kids' hearts and change their lives—forever.

To be a spectacularly successful BibleVenture Buddy, it helps if you...
- love God,
- enjoy being with children,
- can be reflective and thoughtful,
- are comfortable talking with children about Jesus,
- believe children can understand and live God's Word,
- are accepting and supportive of children,
- model God's love in what you say and do, and
- like to laugh and have fun.

Responsibilities

As a BibleVenture Buddy, your responsibilities include...
- attending any scheduled training sessions,
- greeting children as they arrive,
- accompanying your Venture Team when traveling to a Center,
- joining in activities with your Venture Team,
- encouraging the kids in your Venture Team,
- facilitating discussions with your Venture Team,
- actively seeking to grow spiritually and in your leadership skills,
- assisting Center Leaders as needed,
- overseeing the sign-out sheet for your Venture Team, and
- praying for the children you serve.

BibleVenture Center Leader

BibleVenture Center Leaders provide fun, engaging experiences for small groups of kids. Because the focus of each Center is slightly different, the skills required to lead each Center change from Center to Center, too.

But there are a few things *every* effective and successful Center Leader has in common. Successful Center Leader...

- love God,
- enjoy and value children,
- are energetic and upbeat,
- maintain a positive attitude,
- can organize and motivate children to listen,
- are humble,
- are observant,
- attend scheduled leader training,
- prepare lessons thoroughly and with excellence, and
- model God's love in what they say and do.

At the BibleVenture Center program, Leaders serve in these two areas:

1. The Depot

The Depot Leader is the "up front" leader, helping kids transition into BibleVenture by leading a brief, fun, upbeat program.

You're responsible for...

- collecting necessary supplies,
- preparing and leading the weekly openings and closings with excellence,
- reinforcing the daily Bible Point as you lead,
- leading music, or finding someone to help you do so, and
- praying for the children and BibleVenture Buddies you serve.

2. Venture Centers

Center Leaders encourage kids to form a lasting relationship with their BibleVenture Buddies, team members, and Jesus by leading an excellent forty-minute lesson.

You're responsible for...

- collecting necessary supplies,
- preparing and leading the weekly program with excellence,
- reinforcing the daily Bible Point as you lead,
- asking questions that will be discussed among the small groups (not with you!),
- cleaning up your area after your lesson, and
- praying for the children and volunteers in your BibleVenture program.

Job Description: BibleVenture Servant Leader

BibleVenture Servant Leaders support the BibleVenture program by jumping in to help where needed. You have a few assigned tasks but will probably do far more as you're asked to substitute for a missing BibleVenture Buddy, or help out with a drama, or gather supplies, or...

Successful BibleVenture Servant Leaders...

- love God,
- enjoy and value children,
- are energetic and upbeat,
- maintain a positive attitude,
- are humble,
- are observant,
- attend scheduled leader training,
- have servant hearts, and
- model God's love in what they say and do.

Responsibilities

As a BibleVenture Servant Leader, your responsibilities include...

- attending any scheduled training sessions,
- greeting children as they arrive,
- staffing the Depot ticket window during the opening and closing times,
- encouraging kids and leaders,
- actively seeking to grow spiritually and in your leadership skills,
- assisting Center Leaders as needed, and
- praying for the children and leaders in your BibleVenture program.

BibleVenture Sign-In and Sign-Out Sheet

We value the children trusted to our care! Please sign your child in and out. And if there are people who are not permitted to pick up your child, please provide that information to our staff.

CHILD'S NAME:	PERSON SIGNING CHILD IN:	PERSON SIGNING CHILD OUT:	Check if ONLY the person signing child in can sign child out.

Bonus Training Session!

Effective center leaders are made, not born. This one-hour session will help you prepare BibleVenture Center Leaders for their important role in your BibleVenture Centers program.

How to Be a Wildly Successful Venture Center Leader

At the end of this workshop, participants will be able to

- explain their role of Venture Center Leader and
- identify and apply the "Six Habits of Highly Effective Venture Center Leaders."

Supplies

- microphone (if more than 20 people)
- 1 name tag per person
- white board or newsprint
- markers
- 1 copy of the "Job Description: BibleVenture Center Leader" per participant
- 1 pencil or pen per participant
- refreshments

Before the Workshop

Place the white board or newsprint where it will be easily seen by all participants. Make a photocopy of the "Job Description: BibleVenture Center Leader" handout (p. 84) for each participant.

Before people arrive, take time to pray that God will use the information you present to encourage and help your Venture Center Leaders. Ask God to bless them and their ministry to children and adult leaders.

Greet participants warmly as they arrive. Ask each participant to fill in a name tag with his or her first name in capital letters and the name of the Venture Center he or she will lead.

After participants have gathered, ask them to be seated.

SAY **Please pair up with a partner and think back to your elementary school years. Think about the schools you attended and the teachers you had.**

In your mind, picture one of your very favorite teachers. See if you can remember his or her name and what that special teacher looked and sounded like. Remember how you felt about that teacher.

Now turn to your partner and tell him or her a few memories about your special teacher. Why do you remember this teacher so fondly?

Listen to each other carefully because you may be called on to introduce your partner's teacher in a few minutes! You have just over four minutes to share your stories. Begin now.

When two minutes have passed, briefly interject that pairs have another two minutes to share. Suggest that if the second member of each pair hasn't yet started sharing, it's a good time to switch speakers.

After another two minutes pass, ask several people to introduce their partners' favorite teachers, including why the teacher was a favorite. If you have time for everyone to share, do so.

Thank volunteers when they've finished sharing.

SAY **Raise your hand if the teacher you chose was a favorite because he or she taught outstanding class content—you just *loved* his or her sharing about the multiplication tables. Now raise your hand if that teacher was a favorite because he or she somehow connected with you as a person.**

You can expect more hands to go up with the second option you presented.

SAY **Teachers and other children's leaders who deliver great content certainly impact our education. But it's the teachers who *connect* with us who change our lives.**

At our BibleVenture program, we want to deliver great content. We want kids to experience, understand, and apply God's Word. But that's not *all* we want. We want them to learn about and come to *love* God, too. And that takes more than just delivering great content.

As Venture Center Leaders, we're in a great spot to encourage spiritual growth in children in two ways: by delivering fun and involving content, and by encouraging relationships to form and deepen between kids and Christian adults.

Today we'll learn and sharpen skills to help us be more effective as Venture Center Leaders. Let's brainstorm words that describe a wildly successful Venture Center Leader—one who is effective in the role and has fun doing it.

Write "has fun" on a white board or piece of newsprint.

SAY **There's one description I've already mentioned. A wildly successful Venture Center Leader has fun leading—and that makes the job a joy. What are other words we can add to the list?**

Write and affirm suggestions. Probe any suggestions you don't understand with open-ended questions or comments such as "Tell me more about that" or "Help me understand what you mean—what would that look like?"

Write all suggestions legibly and large enough to be seen from the back of the room.

SAY **Great ideas! All these will make us more effective as Venture Center Leaders. I'd like us to focus on four words in particular that will help us be spectacularly successful as Venture Center Leaders.**

But first let's review something you may not have seen for a while—a Venture Center Leader job description.

Give each person a copy of the "Job Description: BibleVenture Center Leader."

Ask a volunteer to read the first two paragraphs aloud. Then ask workshop participants to take turns reading the bulleted items aloud.

When you've finished reading, distribute a pencil to each person.

SAY **Like most job descriptions you see in the paper, this is a description of the *ideal* candidate. Are we all perfect in all these areas? Of course not. We have strengths and weaknesses. Let's each take an honest look at what we consider our strengths and weaknesses as Venture Center Leaders.**

Please circle two items in the list that you think are strong in your life. Draw a line through two items that you think are weaknesses. You have sixty seconds.

When sixty seconds have passed, ask workshop participants to share what they wrote in their pairs.

SAY **We all have places in which we can grow as Venture Center Leaders—me included. And we all have strengths that we can share with our kids and each other. Please join me in a brief prayer.**

PRAY **God, you love children. We know that because when Jesus was most busy with teaching and healing, he made time for children. To Jesus children weren't interruptions; they were people. They weren't discipline problems; they were individuals who needed his attention.**

Thank you for letting us be your children, God. Help us treat the children in our care with the same tenderness and love with which you treat us.

Give us new tools today to use in touching kids' lives for you. We come to you teachable and knowing you have things to teach us.

In Jesus' name, amen.

Four Words

SAY **Here are the four words that describe spectacularly successful Venture Center Leaders. Let's take them one at a time.**

Write these words on the poster paper or white board as you introduce them, or circle where the words already appear on the brainstormed list.

SAY **Spectacularly successful Venture Center Leaders are *servants*. They serve God because of a deep, growing relationship with God, and they serve the children God places in their care. They model God's love in what they say and do.**

Ask pairs to take sixty seconds to brainstorm situations they've experienced or observed in which someone in your church's children's ministry was a servant to kids.

When sixty seconds have passed, ask for one or more pairs to share their stories.

SAY **Spectacularly successful Venture Center Leaders are *flexible*. When things go wrong (and they sometimes will!), these leaders roll with it. They look for ways to turn anything that happens into a learning opportunity. They're willing to make last-minute changes requested by the BibleVentures Director.**

Ask pairs to take sixty seconds to brainstorm situations they've experienced or observed in which someone in your church's children's ministry demonstrated flexibility.

When sixty seconds have passed, ask for one or more pairs to share their stories.

SAY **Spectacularly successful Venture Center Leaders are *focused*. They state and reinforce the Bible Point in ways that are clear and concise. They make sure the time they have with children is a time of fun, learning, and spiritual growth.**

Ask pairs to take sixty seconds to brainstorm situations they've experienced or observed in which someone in your children's ministry has demonstrated an ability to stay focused.

When sixty seconds have passed, ask for one or more pairs to share their stories.

SAY **When it comes to their Christian faith, spectacularly successful Venture Center Leaders are *growing*. They have an authentic, growing**

relationship with God through Christ. They're comfortable talking about Jesus and their Christian faith. Their personal spiritual lives are rich.

Ask pairs to take sixty seconds to brainstorm situations they've experienced or observed in which someone in your church's children's ministry shared an insight that came from personal Bible study or prayer.

When sixty seconds have passed, ask for one or more pairs to share their stories.

SAY **Four things that describe a spectacularly successful Venture Center Leader: A servant who's flexible, focused, and growing in his or her own Christian faith.**

Now let's explore some habits that spectacularly successful Venture Center Leaders form. We'll focus on six of them—so I need six volunteers!

After you've recruited six volunteers, have them stand facing the rest of the group. If you have fewer than six leaders, have everyone stand in a circle and face each other. Starting with the person whose birthday is closest to today, begin going around the circle doing the activity described in the following pages.

Six Habits of Highly Effective Venture Center Leaders

SAY **We all love mimes, right? No? Well, even if we don't, let's take turns being mimes and acting out the following habits! As the habit is discussed, silently act out one way it might show itself at a BibleVenture meeting.**

Read the following descriptions of habits one at a time, allowing time for your mimes to act out something that reflects the habit.

Habit One: *Effective Venture Center Leaders prepare several days in advance.*

SAY **When leaders try to "wing it," it shows. They're glued to their books as they lead. They're unsure of where they're going. They appear nervous, and kids pick up on that uncertainty.**

Leading children is an honor and a holy responsibility. The role deserves excellence, and that doesn't happen if we fail to prepare. The good news is that Venture Centers don't require a great deal of preparation—but they do require *some*. Plan to prepare several days in advance of the next meeting.

Habit Two: *Effective Venture Center Leaders don't make major changes to their activities.*

SAY **If you completely change an activity, you run the risk of duplicating what another center leader will do—or has just done. Plus, activities are carefully arranged to accommodate a variety of learning styles. When you change a game to a lecture, snack, or science project, you've eliminated the opportunity for some learners to connect with the material.**

On the other hand, effective leaders *do* make minor tweaks and adjustments to tailor activities to their circumstances and kids. If you have a particularly large yard, a very small meeting room, or kids with special needs, adjust activities to accommodate your unique situation.

Habit Three: *Effective Venture Center Leaders help BibleVenture Buddies grow closer to children.*

SAY **Your job is to provide experiences that help kids understand and apply the Bible Point. That's one way you serve children.**

Another equally important way you serve is by encouraging kids to connect with their BibleVenture Buddies. That means if you suggest a question for kids to answer, you'll direct kids to answer it *within* their groups.

Whenever possible, you gently direct children to discuss things with their BibleVenture Buddies.

Habit Four: *Effective Venture Center Leaders show up fifteen minutes early.*

SAY **One of the best habits an effective Venture Center Leader can form is the habit of arriving fifteen minutes before kids show up.**

Leaders who arrive early are relaxed and prepared when the program begins. They've already set up supplies and had time to respond if they left something in the car or discovered that, for some reason, the electric plug in their room isn't working. They're ready.

You can use any extra time before the program starts to pray, to talk with other leaders, and to discuss any tweaks in the day's program.

Habit Five: *Effective Venture Center Leaders participate—enthusiastically.*

SAY **During the opening Depot, an effective leader is on hand to applaud, sing, and encourage kids. Effective Venture Center Leaders are active, full participants.**

Effective leaders also stay engaged at their centers while teams debrief activities. These leaders provide "two- and one-minute warnings" to help BibleVenture Buddies keep track of the time. And when they see a BibleVenture Buddy struggling to maintain focus or discipline, effective center leaders come alongside to offer assistance.

Habit Six: *Effective Venture Center Leaders pray for kids and adults daily—not just while at a BibleVenture program.*

SAY **When we pray for the kids and adults who rotate through our Venture Centers, we invite God to do his will and work in their lives. And we make ourselves available if God wants to use us to encourage and bless those precious people.**

Prayer *does* change things—beginning with our hearts for the people we see at every BibleVenture meeting.

Lead a round of applause for your mimes, and ask volunteers to form pairs with someone they haven't yet been partnered with.

SAY **I'm going to read the list of six habits again. As you listen, be looking at the items you circled and crossed off on your handout. If forming one or more of these habits would help you get even better at what you already do**

well, or improve an area of weakness, jot down that habit next to what you've circled or crossed out.

Read through the following:

1. Effective Venture Center Leaders prepare several days in advance.

2. Effective Venture Center Leaders don't make major changes in their activities—but do make minor adjustments.

3. Effective Venture Center Leaders help BibleVenture Buddies form relationships with kids.

4. Effective Venture Center Leaders show up fifteen minutes before kids arrive.

5. Effective Venture Center Leaders participate—enthusiastically.

6. Effective Venture Center Leaders pray for kids daily—not just while at a BibleVenture Center meeting.

Share with your partner one or two of the six habits you'd like to form in your own ministry to kids. What would they help you accomplish more effectively? How could you take a first step in developing these habits? You have five minutes to share.

When time has passed, ask pairs to join together so your leaders are in a large circle.

SAY **One way we model God's love for kids is by supporting and caring about each other. Let's take turns each briefly praying for the person on our right. I'll begin, and we'll go around the circle.**

When you've gone around your circle, close by praying: **Dear God, thank you for the chance to serve you as we serve the children you bring to our BibleVentures program. We want to reflect your love, God. Help us grow in our skills and compassion for kids and their families. In Jesus' name, amen.**

Encourage Venture Center Leaders to stick around for light refreshments. A casual chat time over a cup of coffee allows leaders to continue their discussions and deepen their relationships.

Paul: Shackled and Shipwrecked!

BibleVenture Invitation Letter

Dear Janna,

An earthquake that shatters the walls of a prison, yet no prisoners escape; a man struck blind by a piercing, bright light; dangerous travel to distant lands…

Sounds like a Hollywood movie, doesn't it?

Except this isn't a movie…it's true! And you can learn all about it!

You're invited to join us at *BibleVenture Centers™: Paul—Shackled and Shipwrecked!* each Sunday night starting July 6 at 6.

We'll meet for four Sundays in a row—all July—and you won't want to miss a single night!

Each one-hour program will have you visiting a different BibleVenture Center. One week you may be acting in a fun, no-lines-to-learn drama presentation. Another week you may be crafting an art project to take home. There's always something different, and it's always fun!

Tell your mom or dad right now that you want to join your friends at BibleVenture on July 6! Circle the date on the family calendar! That's the date the adventure begins…and who knows where it will end?

It just might change your life!

Sincerely,

Audrey Ferris
BibleVenture Director,
First Church
555-1212

Invite kids to your **BibleVenture Centers™: Paul—Shackled and Shipwrecked!** *program! Adapt this invitation to fit your schedule and church letterhead, then send a copy to each child in your Sunday school. Post copies on community bulletin boards, and send invitations to neighborhood children who visited your vacation Bible school, too!*

Leader Encouragement Pages

Can you imagine doing a BibleVenture program without volunteer leaders? It wouldn't happen!

So thank your leaders weekly with these four reproducible pages. You have one page for each week of this BibleVenture program.

Each week, make a copy of one page for each of your leaders. Slip copies into envelopes, and send each volunteer an encouraging letter. Make it even more special by jotting a personal note on each copy you send.

The ministry volunteer experts at Group's new Church Volunteer Central (www.churchvolunteercentral.com) report that a leading reason volunteers resign their positions is that volunteers don't feel recognized and appreciated.

You can help your precious children's ministry leaders feel valued by saying "Thanks!" on a regular basis...and these pages will help!

You're the Best!

"Glory belongs to God, whose power is at work in us. By this power he can do infinitely more than we can ask or imagine."

—*Ephesians 3:20 (God's Word)*

When you're serving kids, God is working through you. Thanks for being available and willing to make a difference in the lives of children!

You're the Best!

"Be sure that you live in a way that brings honor to the Good News of Christ. Then whether I come and visit you or am away from you, I will hear good things about you. I will hear that you continue strong with one purpose and that you work together as a team for the faith of the Good News."

—*Philippians 1:27 (International Children's Bible)*

When you lead children, there's never a dull moment...or one when you're "offstage." This week let God's light shine so children can see God's glory reflected in and through you!

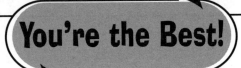

"Dear brothers and sisters, whenever trouble comes your way, let it be an opportunity for joy."

—James 1:2 (New Living Translation)

Busy day that makes it tough to be ready for our next BibleVenture? Pick up the phone and share the challenge with someone on our ministry team so we can pray for you. And let's find joy in your journey!

You're the Best!

"But those who wait upon God get fresh strength. They spread their wings and soar like eagles, they run and don't get tired, they walk and don't lag behind."

—Isaiah 40:31 (The Message)

When you minister to kids this week, be sure to let God work through you. You'll find there's power far beyond what you can muster on your own to be patient, loving, and kind. Look to God for strength today!

How to Connect With Kids

Dear BibleVenture Leader,

For just a moment, think about your favorite teacher in grade school.

Can you remember that person? Picture the teacher's face and—if you can—the classroom where you spent time with that teacher. Fix that face and space in your mind.

Now think about *why* that teacher was your favorite.

I'm willing to bet it wasn't because the teacher was especially good at providing instruction about geography or at teaching the alphabet. While your favorite teacher might have sparkled at his or her teaching skills, it's not likely that's why you connected in such a meaningful way.

Rather, I'm willing to bet that you connected with that teacher *personally*. You had a *relationship* with him or her, and it's that relationship you remember so warmly.

Here's what you probably *don't* remember: Your favorite teacher probably did lots of little things to connect with you, to communicate warmth and caring. Maybe it was tucking a Valentine's Day card in your box or remembering your birthday. Maybe it was simply knowing your name when so many adults didn't bother to learn it.

Whatever those little things were, it's likely that no matter how special that teacher made you feel, he or she did the same things with other students, too.

That's right: *Your* favorite teacher is probably other peoples' favorite teacher! The little habits and connection skills used with you probably endeared your teacher to other kids, too.

It's the little things that count—and connect.

Now think about your role in our BibleVenture program. You have contact with kids week after week, and that means you have the potential to be the teacher someone remembers fondly twenty years from now when picturing a face from the past.

That's right—*you* can be that children's leader who has such a huge impact on a child that you're remembered long after the child has become an adult.

To do that you'll need to do your job well at BibleVenture, but you'll need to do something more.

You'll need to connect with kids.

I want to suggest three "little things" that will go a long way toward connecting you with kids. They're habits you can easily develop, and they'll cost you nothing...but they'll give kids a bridge into a relationship with you.

How to Connect With Kids

1. Be approachable.

Ever talk with someone standing on a stepladder or on steps? Uncomfortable, isn't it?

That's what it's like for children to talk with adults, especially tall ones. Kids crane their necks and strain to hear what grown-ups are saying. And then there's the "other challenge": what to call you.

Here are some easy ways to be approachable to children...

● *Kneel when you're talking with kids.* This removes the obstacle of your height difference and lets you engage children in eye-to-eye conversation.

● *Be cheerful—and smile.* When adults appear grumpy or angry, children often wonder if it's their fault. So be deliberate about leaving your disgust with the crack in your car windshield out in the parking lot with your car. When you enter the room for BibleVenture, be smiling and welcoming.

● *Wear a name tag.* This not only helps children remember your name but also signals how you want to be addressed. If you write, "Mrs. Smith," that's what kids will call you. But if you write, "Sally," that gives children permission to call you by your first name.

● *Use children's name in conversations.* If your memory is wired so names escape you, go to the trouble of having kids wear name tags. Or simply make it important enough to learn names.

● *Wear comfortable clothing that lets you enter into activities.* In any given BibleVenture program, your kids might be painting, skipping, or pretending they're in an earthquake as they roll around on the floor. Be dressed so you can join them!

2. Share your life—within reason.

Grown-ups lead lives that are completely different from lives lived by children. It's like we're on different planets. That's why it's critical that, in a healthy way, you share what's happening in your life.

Because kids aren't your peers, you need to be careful about what you share. Never make a child uncomfortable or responsible for more information than he or she can bear.

That still leaves plenty of material that's appropriate to discuss—your family, for instance, or upcoming travel plans. General health issues might be appropriate, too, and work- or school-related topics.

Here are several simple ways to share your life with your children...

● **When it's prayer time, share something.** Asking children to pray for you and your life communicates that you value both prayer and your kids.

● *Bring in a picture of your family to pass around.* Maybe it's your husband and kids, your parents, or even a candid picture of your dog (do they take formal dog photos?). It doesn't matter what the photo is; the fact that you're passing it around gives children a sense that you live in the real world. You're not just the person they see at church.

3. Have fun.

The children's version of that famous saying reads this way: "The families that play together, stay together."

At our BibleVenture we're trying to build a family atmosphere. That's why children are in small groups with consistent adult leadership. That's why we encourage relationship-building.

And what do they call the person in a family who never enters into games or parties? A *party pooper*, that's what!

Don't be a party pooper. Dive into activities with your kids as your playmates. Your participation gives you a shared experience with the kids and provides a richer, more authentic debriefing time after visiting Venture Centers.

Here are some ways to have fun with children...

● *Check your dignity at the door.* OK, maybe you don't particularly want to stick your hands in paint and leave a handprint on a banner. So what? Do it anyway, and enter into the spirit of the moment alongside your kids. Sing along even if you don't sing well. Play the game even if you know you won't win. Play a part in the drama even if you know there's no Academy Award in your future.

● *Participate in everything.* That means the snack, the skits, the games... everything. If you give yourself permission to opt out of some activities, your kids will do the same. Your participation sets the standard—make sure that standard is "we do it all." If you're not participating, there's no chance for you to have fun with your kids!

● *Don't be competitive.* If you feel you should make a good showing because you're the grown-up, get over it. Relax and enjoy yourself, and consider it all joy should a child beat you across the finish line in the toe-to-heel relay.

After all, is winning that race really so important for your career advancement? A high score for you means nothing; to a child it's what makes a great day.

How to Connect With Kids

How hard is it to connect with kids in a significant, life-changing way?

It takes a decision that kids are important, and your volunteering to serve at BibleVenture shows you've already decided that.

It takes a childlike (not *childish*) heart and willingness to let others in.

And it takes placing good connection habits into your daily life and ministry. You can start with those identified above, but they're just the tip of the iceberg. Watch adults who kids love, and you'll find more and more behaviors that tear down barriers and build bridges instead. Plug those behaviors into our own ministry style; you'll see kids warm up to you even more.

God bless you as you serve kids. You're doing work that will change lives—the lives of your kids and your own life, too!

Make a copy of this letter for each of your BibleVenture volunteers!

Tips From the Trenches for BibleVenture Buddies

"I have a child who absolutely refuses to write or draw in his visa. And when I insist, he doodles and draws tanks. What do I do?"

Be aware that there are children who dislike writing and drawing, and nothing you say or do will change that.

Visas are a tool for helping kids remember the lessons and reinforce the Bible truth. If a child won't use the visa, try to accomplish those purposes without it. Pair up with this child and talk through the questions in the visa. Help this child see value in the process by engaging in it yourself.

And at bare minimum, you *can* insist that kids who choose to not participate don't distract others.

"Hey, what if I want to tell kids more about the Bible—to show them verses that will help them grow spiritually? Can I do that?"

Of course. There are times it's absolutely appropriate for you to speak God's truth into a situation. But think of how you feel when you're talking with a friend about something you're thinking through and your friend suddenly starts handing out advice. How does that feel?

Kids get that *all* the time—especially from adults. What they *most* need to do is grow in their relationship with God, so keep focused on that.

Plus, BibleVenture Centers deliberately seeks to take a simple Bible truth and plant it deep in kids' hearts and minds. That doesn't happen instantly. If it takes a few weeks and the kids truly grasp the significance of a Bible truth, it's worth the time investment.

You can clutter the process if you insist on dealing with a dozen Scripture passages lightly rather than one in depth.

Sometimes less is truly more.

"We use BibleVenture Centers during a midweek slot. Some of my leaders bring their own kids, and some parents drop off their kids a half hour before we get started. What do I do with those kids while we're waiting to get going?"

You can't overestimate the value of a special box full of easy-to-play group games like beanbags, Tick-Tack-Toe, and ball toss. Kids who arrive early take their pick of these games as music plays in the background. A few minutes before the opening Depot program, put the games away.

BibleVenture Buddies can join in the games, or just let the kids play together.

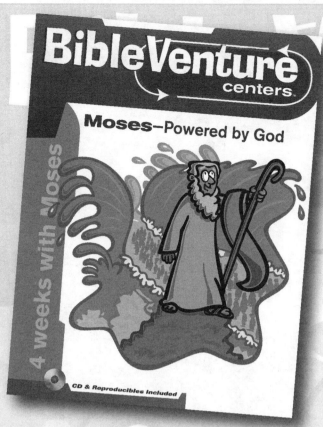

Moses—Powered by God

4 weeks with Moses

CD & Reproducibles Included

Your kids will explore how God used Moses, and discover how God can use them, too...at *Moses—Powered by God!*

Venture Verse

"Cast your cares on the Lord and he will sustain you" *(Psalm 55:22).*

At ***Moses—Powered by God!*** kids visit four Venture Centers...

● *The Music Center* where kids explore instruments, discover how to make sounds that remind them of Moses' life, and along the way they learn God used Moses...and God can use them, too!

● *The Arts & Crafts Center* where they'll discover the early years of Moses as they craft Baby Moses figures and floating baskets.

The Drama Center

● *The Drama Center* where they'll explore the life of Moses and discover that just like God used Moses, God can use them, too!

The Games Center

● *The Games Center* where kids will play games that teach them all about the plagues visited on the Egyptians.

Group

Order today at www.group.com
or call 1-800-747-6060 ext.1370

At BibleVenture your children won't just learn God's Word...they'll *experience* it!

FaitHWeaVeR **FRienDS**

See KiDS

Adventures in faith, actions, and outreach!

It's a ReVoLutionary **MiDWeeK PROGRam** foR KiDS...

a fantastic **FaitH JouRney**...

Group